THE BOOK OF PRESIDENTS

by
Orville V. Webster III

1

JBG PUBLISHING
Los Angeles
Printed in the United States
All Rights Reserved

TABLE OF CONTENTS

GEORGE WASHINGTON
1st President of the United States, 1789-1797
"Father of his Country"

Born: February 22, 1732, Fredricksburg, VA
Died: December 14, 1799, Mount Vernon, VA

George Washington, the eldest of six children from his father's second marriage, was born into the landed gentry in 1732 at Wakefield plantation, Virginia. He lived there and at other plantations along the Potomac and Rappahannock Rivers, including the one that later became known as Mount Vernon, until the age of 16.

George spent much of his boyhood outdoors, growing tall and lean with fair skin that sunburned easily. He became an excellent horseman.

After losing his father when he was 11 years old, George's half-brother Lawrence became his mentor. At 15 George accompanied a party of surveyors to the Shenandoah Valley. He later worked as public surveyor of Fairfax County, Virginia. When he was 21 years old, his military career began when the Royal Governor appointed him to an adjutantship in the militia. That same year, as a gubernatorial emissary, he traveled to Fort Le Boef, Pennsylvania, in the Ohio River Valley, and delivered an ultimatum to French authorities to end their fortification and settlement in British territory.

In 1755, Washington was the aide-de-camp to British General Edward Braddock, who was leading a small army that sought to challenge French control of the Ohio River Valley. The British general knew very little about fighting in the wilderness, marching his troops straight into an ambush. However, during the defeat Washington's cool courageousness demonstrated the qualities of a first-rate officer. He was not hurt, but two horses were killed from under him and his uniform was slashed by four bullets. It was largely due to Washington's leadership that part of the British Army escaped. As a reward for his bravery, Washington was made a colonel and placed in command of the Virginia militia forces. For the next several years he led his troops in small frontier fights against the French and the Indians.

Washington married Martha Dandridge Custis, a wealthy widow and mother of two children, in 1759. The couple had no children of their own, but Washington raised those of his wife as his own. Over the next 15 years, he managed his plantations — including tobacco, horses, cattle, apples, pears, and peaches — and sat in the Virginia House of Burgesses, where he supported the initial protests against British policies.

Washington represented Virginia at the First and Second Continental Congresses. In 1775, after the fighting broke out at Lexington and Concord, he was appointed Commander in Chief of the Continental Army. Overcoming severe obstacles, he eventually put together a well-trained and disciplined fighting force.

Although his army lost more battles than it won, it was never destroyed, and it was never captured. Washington always claimed that as long as the Americans could keep an army in the field, the British could not defeat them. Somehow Washington kept his army in the field, persevering even during the dark winters at Valley Forge, Pennsylvania, and Morristown, New Jersey. He had an unusual ability to inspire men, making them feel that as long as he led them they could not lose. Finally, with the help of the French fleet and army, he won a climactic victory at the Battle of Yorktown, Virginia, in 1781.

After the signing of the Treaty of Paris (1783), Washington resigned his commission and returned to Mount Vernon. His retirement, however, was to be brief. He hosted the Mount Vernon conference (1785) at his estate after the initial meetings in Alexandria, Virginia. In 1786, he presided over the Constitutional Convention, whose success was profoundly influenced by his presence. Following the Constitution's ratification, the electoral college unanimously chose Washington as the nation's first president.

Prior to his inauguration, while he was still the Commander in Chief of the Continental Army, an attempt was made to kidnap or kill Washington. Involved in the conspiracy were the Tory Governor of New York, William Tryon, the Tory Mayor of New York city, David Matthews, and many others, including Thomas Hickey, one of Washington's bodyguards. Hickey was later found guilty, and on June 28, 1776, he was hanged on a field near the Bowery Lane in the presence of 20,000 people.

On April 30, 1789, after a celebratory journey from Mount Vernon to New York City, Washington took the oath of office at Federal hall. The President believed the as the Chief Officer of a new nation, he should present a dignified appearance. Accordingly, Washington dressed in very formal attire; he traveled in a handsome carriage pulled by beautiful horses.

During his two terms, Washington displayed a belief that the government should not be divided and run by political parties. He thought his job was to be President of all the people. Thus, he set about reconciling competing factions and divergent policies within the government and his administration.

During Washington's tenure, the government moved from New York to Philadelphia (1790), and he supervised the planning for relocation to the District of Columbia. Washington laid the cornerstone of the Capitol in 1793.

Although the public encouraged Washington to

seek a third term, he had grown tired of politics and refused to run again. In his "Farewell Address" (1796), he urged his fellow countrymen to renounce party spirit and sectional passions and to avoid involvement in the wars and domestic affairs of other nations.

On December 12, 1799, Washington became sick when he was caught in a snowstorm while riding a horse around his farm. Two days later he died at the age of 67.

On December 26, 1799, General Henry Lee, father of General Robert E. Lee, gave his "Funeral Oration Upon George Washington" before the houses of Congress. During this speech, Lee claimed that Washington was "a citizen first in war, first in peace, first in the hearts of his countrymen."

JOHN ADAMS
2nd President of the United States, 1797-1801
"Father of the United States Navy"

Born: October 30, 1735, Braintree, MA
Died: July 4, 1826, Braintree, MA

John Adams was born on a small farm near what is now Quincy, Massachusetts. The eldest of three sons, he graduated from Harvard College in 1755, and for a short while taught school at Worcester, Massachusetts. After considering entering the ministry, Adams decided to study law.

In 1758, Adams was admitted to the bar. That same year he took an M.A. degree at Harvard, and began to practice in his hometown. Six years later, he married Abigail Smith, who was to give birth to three sons — one of whom was John Quincy — and two daughters. She thus became the only woman in U.S. history to be the wife of one President and the mother of another.

As was the case with many of his contemporaries, Adams was propelled into the Revolutionary camp by the Stamp Act. In 1768 he achieved recognition throughout the Colonies for defending John Hancock, whom British customs officials had charged with smuggling.

Adams soon became one of the leaders of the American Independence movement. He was a member of the Continental Congress from 1774 to 1778, chairing 25 of the more than 90 congressional committees on which he sat. He played an instrumental role in obtaining Washington's appointment as Commander in Chief of the Continental Army, and was a member of the five man committee charged with drafting the Declaration of Independence. Adams then led the debate in Congress to have the declaration passed.

In 1778, Adams wrote a constitution for his home state of Massachusetts; it would later serve as one of the models for the Constitution of the United States. In 1783, he joined Benjamin Franklin and John Jay in negotiating the Treaty of Paris (1783), whereby Britain recognized the independence of the United States.

In 1789, Adams was elected as the nation's first Vice President (1789-97). When Washington refused to run for a third term, Adams was elected President, with his arch enemy Thomas Jefferson as his Vice President.

Because France and England were at war, Adams asked Congress to order new warships. He established a Navy department for the first time, for which he is sometimes called the "Father of the United States Navy." While the Federalists wanted war with France, the statesmanlike Adams insisted on remaining neutral, finally winning an amicable peace. By saving his country from war, Adams angered the leaders of the

Federalist party. In the election of 1801 they turned against him and he was defeated.

Near the end of Adams' term as President, the government moved from Philadelphia to the new capital city of Washington, D.C. Adams retired to "Peacefield," Massachusetts. He lived to see his son John Quincy become president, eventually dying at the age of 90 — just a few hours after Thomas Jefferson — on July 4, 1826. Ironically, it was the 50th anniversary of the adoption of the Declaration of Independence.

THOMAS JEFFERSON
3rd President of the United States, 1801-1809
"Author of the Declaration of Independence"

Born: April 13, 1743, Goochland County, VA
Died: July 4, 1826, Charlottesville, VA

Thomas Jefferson was born in 1743 at Shadwell, a frontier plantation in Goochland (Albemarle) County, Virginia. When his father, Peter, died in 1757, Thomas inherited nearly 3,000 acres of land.

Jefferson, who had one of the most brilliant minds in American history, was tall and thin with a freckled face and sandy hair. In 1762, at the age of 19, he graduated from the College of William and Mary. Before he was 30 years old he had studied half a dozen languages, law (he was admitted to the bar in 1767), mathematics, philosophy, and science. A self-taught architect, he designed some of the most beautiful homes in the world. As an inventor, he created the American system of money.

When he was 26 years old, Jefferson was elected to the Virginia legislature, where he was to write many letters and articles about the growing conflict between the Colonies and Great Britain. His opposition to England became so strong that the British declared him a traitor to be hanged once he was seized.

In 1772 he married Martha Wayles Skelton, a

widow. During their decade of life together, she was to bear six children. Three years later he was elected to the Continental Congress. In 1776, because of his fame as a writer, the 33 year old Jefferson was assigned to the five-man committee chosen to write the Declaration of Independence, a task his associates subsequently delegated to him.

After the war, Jefferson succeeded Benjamin Franklin as Minister to France (1785-89). When the new Constitution was adopted and George Washington was elected President, Jefferson was appointed Secretary of State (1790-93).

During Jefferson's tenure as Secretary of State, he often feuded with Alexander Hamilton on most aspects of natonal policy. Jefferson sympathized with the French Revolution. He opposed a strong central government, instead favoring states' rights. Hamilton took the opposite position on these issues. Soon, such political and philosophical conflicts resulted in the formation of the Federalist Party and the Democratic-Republican Party, which Jefferson co-founded with James Madison. In 1793, because of Washington's growing reliance on Hamilton for advice on foreign affairs, Jefferson resigned as Secretary of State.

In 1796, Jefferson lost the presidential election to Federalist John Adams by only three electoral votes. However, because the Constitution did not yet provide separate tickets for the President and Vice Presdent, Jefferson became Vice President (1797-1801), despite the fact that he was a member of the opposing party.

In 1800, after a tie-breaking election in the Federalist-controlled House of Representatives, Jefferson captured the Presidency, while his opponent Aaron Burr became Vice President. Jefferson was the first President to take the oath of office in Washington, D.C.

On July 4, 1801, President Jefferson held a reception in the Blue Room at the White House, where he introduced the custom of shaking his guests' hands rather than bowing stiffly, a custom observed by Presidents Washington and Adams.

In 1804, Jefferson was elected for a second term.

Jefferson's greatest achievements were in the area of westward expansion. Believing that the future of the United States lay in the West, Jefferson sent his diplomats to Paris to draw up the details of the Louisiana Purchase (1803), which doubled the size of the United States and extended its boundaries beyond the Mississippi River to the Rocky Mountains. Additionally, he sent the Lewis and Clark expedition (1804-6) to the Pacific.

Jefferson refused to be elected to a third term because he did not believe that any man should be President for more than two terms. He went back to his beautiful home, Monticello ("little mountain"), where he corresponded with and entertained statesmen, politicians, scholars, scientists, explorers, and Indian chiefs. Jefferson also planned and helped build the University of Virginia. Falling into debt, the former President was forced to sell his library to the Government. This eventually became the nucleus of the Library of Congress.

Jefferson died on the same day as John Adams, July 4, 1826 — exactly 50 years after the adoption of the Declaration of Independence. Jefferson wrote the words to go on his gravestone: "Here was buried Thomas Jefferson, author of the Declaration of Independence, of the statute of Virginia for religious freedom, and father of the University of Virginia." Oddly, he did not mention having been President of the United States.

JAMES MADISON
4th President of the United States, 1809-1817
"Father of the Constitution"

Born: March 16, 1751, Port Conway, VA
Died: June 28, 1836, Montpelier, VA

James Madison, a gaunt, sickly child, was born in 1751 at Port Conway, King George County, Virginia. However, most of James Madison's youth was spent at the Montpelier estate, in Orange County, Virginia. Though frail at only five and a half feet tall and weighing about 100 pounds, Madison was an excellent student, graduating in only two years from the College of New Jersey (Princeton University) in 1771.

After considering a career in the ministry, Madison opted for politics and in 1775 he served on the Orange County Comittee of Safety. The following year, as a member of the Virginia Convention, he helped to frame the Virginia constitution.

Because of his poor health, Madison never served in the military. However, in 1780 he was chosen to represent Virginia in the Continental Congress (1780-83 and 1786-88). During this period, he urged that a convention be called to form a central government. And at the Constitutional Convention in the summer of 1787, his Virginia Plan became the primary basis for the

Constitution, earning him the title, "Father of the Constitution." Additionally, his journal of the convention remains the most complete record of the event.

After the new government had been formed, Madison served in the House of Representatives from 1789 to 1797, where he helped frame and pass the Bill of Rights. As one of the leaders of the opposition to Alexander Hamilton's policies, he helped found the Democratic-Republican Party.

In 1794, when he was 43 years old, Madison married a vivacious widow, Dorothea ("Dolley") Payne. While they made an odd-looking couple — the pretty Dolley was 16 years the junior of the thin, sick-looking, middle-aged Madison — they were an extremely happy couple.

In 1801 Thomas Jefferson appointed Madison as Secretary of State. Madison served for eight years, and when Jefferson retired Madison was elected President in 1809.

Madison immediately had to deal with the ramifications of European wars. When his diplomatic solutions failed to prevent the seizure of U.S. ships, goods, and men on the high seas, Madison succumbed to pressure from "The War Hawks," and in 1812, agreeing that U.S. honor and economic independence were at stake, he asked Congress to declare war against Britain.

The war effort did not go well in the beginning.

Poor generalship, inadequate troop strength, and supply and transportation problems led to the defeat of American armies along the Canadian border. At sea, despite a few brilliant victories, the U.S. Navy could not stand up to the Royal Navy, which blockaded the coast. On August 24, 1814, the British captured Washington, D.C., burned the White House and the Capitol building, and forced the members of the Government to flee the city. Unable to understand just how defenseless the Capitol was, the British officers feared they were being drawn into a trap. Thus, afraid of being cut off from their base and their supplies, they retreated, thus ending the rout and saving the city from even greater destruction.

While victories at Chesapeake Bay — which provided the inspiration for Francis Scott Key's "The Star-Spangled Banner" — and New Orleans led many Americans to believe that the United States had won the war, the conflict ended in a stalemate when the inconclusive Treaty of Ghent was signed.

After the end of his second term, Madison retired to his home in Virginia. He later served as co-chairman of the Virginia Constitutional Convention of 1829-30 and as rector of the University after 1826. He passed away at the age of 85 in 1836, the last surviving signer of the Constitution.

JAMES MONROE
5th President of the United States, 1817-1825
"The Monroe Doctrine"

Born: April 28, 1758, Westmoreland County, VA
Died: July 4, 1831, New York, NY

The son of a modest farmer and the oldest of five children, James Monroe was born in 1758 in Westmoreland County, Virginia. Tall and raw-boned with a quiet dignity, Monroe left home at the age of 16 to attend William and Mary College. Two years later, in 1776, he left college early to join the Continental Army. During his four years of service, Monroe was wounded twice. Upon his discharge as a major in 1780, he studied law with Thomas Jefferson, who became his lifelong friend and advisor.

In 1782, when Monroe was only 24, he was elected to the Virginia Legislature. The following year, he began a stint in the Continental Congress (1783-86). In 1786, he married Elizabeth Kortright, who was to bear two daughters and a son.

In 1790, the Virginia legislature appointed Monroe to the U.S. Senate. Service as Minister to France (1794-96) and Governor of Virginia (1799-1802) soon followed. In 1803 he aided Robert R. Livingston in negotiations with France which resulted in the Louisiana Purchase.

After an unsuccessful bid for the Presidency in

1808, Monroe became Madison's Secretary of State (1811-17), and Secretary of War (1814-15).

In 1816, Monroe was elected President — the last of the Revolutionary leaders to become Chief Executive — initiating the "Era of Good Feelings." This state of the Union ended, however, when a depression struck the country in 1819 and, as if that weren't bad enough, sectional debates erupted in Congress when Missouri sought admission to the Union as a slave state. Disaster was averted with the Missouri Compromise (1820), which admitted Missouri as a slave state and Maine as a free state while outlawing slavery in the Louisiana Purchase area north and west of the southern boundary of Missouri.

In 1820 Monroe was elected to a second term as President. He received every vote in the electoral college except one — the lone exception being from a man who said he did not think anybody but George Washington should ever receive all of the votes.

Monroe's greatest diplomatic accomplishment occurred in 1823, when Spain asked the help of France and other European countries to reconquer the newly freed countries of South America. President Monroe did not want any intrusions in the area, declaring that no new colonies were to be started in the Americas. This became known as the Monroe Doctrine, and it has since become one of the cornerstones of U.S. foreign policy.

When his second term ended, Monroe returned to his home in Virginia. He died on July 4, 1831, after moving to New York to live with one of his daughters. He was 73 years old. Of the five Presidents who took part in the Revolution, three of them — Thomas Jefferson, John Adams, and James Monroe — died on a Fourth of July.

JOHN QUINCY ADAMS
5th President of the United States, 1825-1829
"Old Man Eloquent"

Born: July 11, 1767, Quincy, MA
Died: February, 23, 1848, Washington, D.C.

John Quincy Adams, the son of John Adams, second President of the United States, was born in 1767 at Braintree (later Quincy), Massachusetts. A precocious child, John Quincy spent the years 1778 to 1785 in Europe, where his father served as American diplomat. Formally educated in France, Germany, and Holland, John Quincy quickly achieved exceptional maturity for his age. When he was only 14 years old he went to Russia to serve as secretary for the first U.S. diplomatic agent in that country. The following year he worked as secretary for his father, who was helping to write the Treaty of 1783, which ended the American Revolution.

Returning to the United States in 1785, Adams attended Harvard University, where he graduated in 1787. After practicing law for a few years, Adams was sent by President Washington to represent the United States in several European countries.

In 1802, after failing to win election to the U.S. House of Representatives, Adams entered the State Senate, soon followed by service in the U.S.

Senate (1803-8). President Madison sent Adams to Europe in 1814 to help negotiate the Treaty of Ghent, which ended the War of 1812. He subsequently served as Minister to Britain from 1815 to 1817, and when James Monroe became President in 1817, He appointed Adams as Secretary of State.

Adams became one of the truly great Secretaries of State in U.S. history. He helped settle a quarrel between the United States and England over the Oregon Territory. He was instrumental in the acquisition of Florida from Spain, earned Spanish recognition of U.S. claims to the Pacific Northwest, arranged for the joint Anglo-American occupancy of Oregon, and helped frame the Monroe Doctrine.

In 1824, Adams was elected to the Presidency, the only son of a Chief Executive to become President himself. While Andrew Jackson had received the most electoral votes, none of the four candidates running for the office obtained the required majority. When Henry Clay, who had drawn the least number of votes and disliked Jackson intensely, threw his support to Adams, John Quincy won the election. Upon Adams' appointment of Clay as Secretary of State, Jackson's followers charged that the two had made a "corrupt bargain."

Adams' four years as President were certainly the most unhappy time of his life. His sharp tongue made enemies, and he was an extremely lonely man. His ideas, which included the building of a comprehensive system of roads and canals, a high protective tariff to stimulate manufacturing, Government encouragement of the arts and sciences, the establishment of a national university, and the financing of scientific expeditions, were turned down by Congress. In the mudslinging election of 1828, he was soundly defeated by rival Andrew Jackson.

Stung by his harsh defeat, Adams returned to "Peacefield," Massachusetts. But when the people of his area elected him to the House of Representatives, he began a distinguished 17 year career (1831-48) as the only ex-President to serve in Congress. He helped establish the Smithsonian Institution, protested the Mexican War (1846-48), favored the standardization of weights and measures, and fought against slavery and for civil rights and free speech. During a debate in the speaker's room in the House of Representatives on February 21, 1848, the 80-year old Adams suffered a stroke and died 2 days later.

ANDREW JACKSON
7th President of the United States, 1829-1837
"Old Hickory"

Born: March 15, 1767, Waxhaw Settlement, SC
Died: June 8, 1845, Nashville, TN

Andrew Jackson was the first President born in a log cabin. His mother and father had come from Ireland in 1765, only two years before his birth. He never knew his father, who died in an accident about 2 weeks before he was born, while his mother died when he was only 14 years old.

Andrew had very little formal education to speak of, but he learned to read from his brothers and an uncle who looked after him. At the age of nine years old he read the Declaration of Independence aloud to a group of frontiersmen. When some of these same frontiersmen formed a Revolutionary Army unit, Andrew watched as they practiced and drilled. At the age of 13 he joined the army himself, carrying messages from one unit to another. A year later he and his brother were captured by the British. One day, when Jackson refused to clean an English officer's boots, he was cut across the head; the blow left a scar on his face, and resulted in his permanent hatred of the British.

After the war, Jackson studied law in Salisbury, North Carolina. In 1790 he became Attorney

General of the Western District of North Carolina (now Tennessee). Jackson married Rachel Donelson Robards in 1791, but the ceremony had to be repeated several years later because of a legal technicality in Rachel's divorce from her first husband. This slight blemish provided plenty of firepower for Jackson's political enemies throughout his career.

Tall, handsome, and gregarious, Jackson thoroughly enjoyed life on the frontier. A gambler, he wagered on horses, cockfights, and business. His own personal economic situation was like a roller coaster — he made money, lost it, and made it again. Reckless and quick-tempered, he was twice wounded in duels, and is believed to have participated in approximately 100 duels during his lifetime.

There are detailed records of one such duel. Charles Dickinson, known to be one of the most skillful pistol shots in the United States, apparently made some derogatory remarks about Mrs. Jackson, after which Andrew Jackson quickly challenged him to a duel. They met on May 30, 1806, at Harrison's Mill on Red River in Logan County, Kentucky. At the signal, Dckinson fired first, breaking some of Jackson's ribs and grazing his breastbone. However, Jackson, without flinching, maintained his position and fired, killing Dickinson with one shot.

In 1796 Jackson served as Tennessee's first U.S.

Representative (1796-97), U.S. Senator (1797-98), and Judge of the State Superior Court (1798-1804). When the people in Tennessee raised an army to fight the Creek Indians in 1802, Jackson was elected a major general in the Tennessee militia. While he had had no military training, he proved to be an excellent general, defeating the Creek Indians at the Battle of Horseshoe Bend, Alabama (1814). The following year, Jackson was made a general in the Federal Army. In the last battle of the War of 1812 he led his motley army to a victory over the British Regulars at the Battle of New Orleans and became a national hero.

In 1817 Jackson led U.S. forces in the First Seminole War (1817-18) and, exceeding his instructions, went on to invade Spanish West Florida. After the U.S. acquired Florida by treaty in 1821, he served as its first Territorial Governor. In 1823 he was reelected to the U.S. Senate from Tennessee.

In 1824 Jackson was defeated by John Quincy Adams in a highly controversial election for President. During the mud-slinging campaign of 1828, Jackson's backers painted him as a military hero, frontiersman, and champion of the average man. To the citizens who were moving west, searching for new land and a new life, Jackson was a hero. He was subsequently swept into office.

A strong, authoritative, and independent leader, he was decisively reelected in 1832. While Jackson had many faults — a belief in slavery and a hatred of the Indians among them — perhaps no man has ever made the office of the President so strong.

Jackson suffered the first attempt upon the life of a President on January 30, 1835, in the rotunda of the Capitol. While Jackson was attending the funeral services for Representative Warren Ransom Davis of South Carolina, Richard Lawrence, a mentally unbalanced house painter, fired two shots at him from a distance of only six feet. Both pistols misfired and Jackson was unhurt.

Nearly deaf, blind in one eye, and suffering the harsh effects from various illnesses and wounds that had plagued him during the course of his life, Jackson died in 1845.

MARTIN VAN BUREN
8th President of the United States, 1837-1841
"Red Fox of Kinderhook"

Born: December 5, 1782, Kinderhook, NY
Died: July 24, 1862, Kinderhook, NY

Martin Van Buren was the first President born after the United States became an independent nation. His father was a tavernkeeper and farmer. After attending local Kinderhook schools for several years, Van Buren began studying law at the age of 14. In 1803 he was admitted to the bar, and in 1807 he married Hannah Hoes, with whom he had four sons before she died 12 years later. He never remarried.

Between the years 1803 and 1820, Van Buren held the offfices of Surrogate of Columbia County, State Senator, and State Attorney General. In 1821, he was elected to the U.S. Senate (1821-28).

In 1827, Van Buren, who by then had earned the nickname the "Little Magician" because of his small size and uncanny political abilities, resigned from the Senate and became Governor of New York. After only 3 months, however, he resigned when Jackson was elected President and he was offered the position of Secretary of State (1829-31). He went on to become Jackson's most trusted advisor.

When Jackson ran for a second term, he asked Van Buren to be his Vice President. In 1836, with the help of Jackson, Van Buren was elected to the Presidency.

At this point, the nation entered the Panic of 1837, one of the worst economic depressions in the history of the country. Van Buren was easy to blame. A dapper dresser who was known to live the good life, Van Buren's enemies claimed that he drank foreign wines and used gold forks and silver plates. Details such as these were enough to make hungry people without jobs vote against Van Buren, and in the election of 1840 he was defeated by William Henry Harrison.

In 1844, Van Buren was defeated in a bid for the Democratic Presidential nomination. In 1848 Van Buren again ran for President, this time receiving no electoral votes. He died in 1862 at the age of 79.

WILLIAM HENRY HARRISON
9th President of the United States, 1841
"Old Tippecanoe"

Born: February 9, 1773, Berkeley Plantation, VA
Died: April 4, 1841, Washington, D.C.

William Henry Harrison's father was the son of Benjamin Harrison, a former Governor of Virginia who signed the Declaration of Independence. When he was 14 years old, Harrison attended Hampden-Sidney College. While he studied the Greek and Latin classics voraciously, he did not graduate. Instead, upon his father's death in 1791, Harrison quit school and accepted a commission as an ensign in the Army. For several years he served on the northwest frontier, fighting against the Indians.

Harrison next served as the Secretary of the Northwest Territory, and in 1800, at the age of 27, President John Adams appointed him as Governor of the Indiana Territory (1801-12).

In 1811, while attempting to suppress a confederation led by the Shawnee chief, Harrison's forces burned the town near Tippecanoe Creek. Although the battle was celebrated as a great victory and made Harrison a national hero, it actually proved to be indecisive and military losses were heavy.

After the war, Harrison was elected as a U.S. Representative (1816-19), State Senator (1819-21), U.S. Senator (1825-28), and Minister to Colombia (1828-29).

In 1840, during what became known as the "log cabin and hard cider campaign," Harrison ran against Martin Van Buren in the Presidential election. Harrison, painted as the hero of Tippecanoe, ran under the slogan "Tippecanoe and Tyler, too." In a circus-like campaign, the aristocratic Harrison was portrayed as a log cabin-dwelling, hard-cider-drinking frontiersman who was a major military hero. Van Buren, on the other hand, was branded as a champagne-drinking dandy. Harrison easily defeated his opponent.

At his inauguration, Harrison rode a white horse to the Capitol, refusing to wear a hat or coat despite the cold and stormy weather. His 8,578-word inaugural address — the longest on record — took about one hour and forty-five minutes to read. During the ceremony, Harrison caught cold. He died of pneumonia at the age of 68 on April 4, 1841. He is thus remembered for having the shortest term of all the Presidents.

JOHN TYLER
10th President of the United States, 1841-1845

"His Accidency"

Born: March 29, 1790, Greenway, VA
Died: January 18, 1862, Richmond, VA

John Tyler was born in Charles City County, Virginia in 1790, the second son and sixth child of eight in a distinguished Virginia planter family. His mother died when he was only seven years of age.

Tyler graduated from the College of William and Mary when he was 17, was admitted to the bar two years later, and at the age of 21 was elected to the Virginia Legislature. In 1813 he married Letitia Christian, who was to bear eight children — three sons and five daughters, before her death in 1842.

Tyler's distinguished political career included a run as a member of the U.S. House of Representatives (1816-21), another stint in the Virginia House of Delegates (1823-25), a term as Governor (1825-27), and nine years as a U.S. Senator (1827-36).

The Whig party nominated Tyler for Vice President in 1840 in order to broaden the appeal of their ticket. Presidential nominee Harrison was from the West, and the Whigs wanted a Vice

President who could help get the Southern vote. Tyler, a Southerner and a Democrat, seemed to be the perfect choice.

But when President Harrison died suddenly, the Whigs had to reckon with "Tyler, too," at that point the youngest President (at 51 years old) ever to be inaugurated, as well as the first Vice President elevated to the Presidency through the death of a Chief Executive.

Tyler's wife died soon after he became President and he married again, becoming the first President whose wife died while he was in office. His second wife, Julia Gardiner, was thirty years younger than he was. Together they had five sons and two daughters.

When Tyler demanded to be regarded as a duly-elected President rather than as the acting Chief Executive, the Whigs — mostly Northerners and Westerners — still hoped he would adopt their programs. But Tyler disagreed with most Whig ideas. When he vetoed a national bank bill for the second time, all of his Cabinet members (with the exception of Secretary of State Daniel Wester) resigned.

Despite such difficulties, Tyler accomplished a great deal in foreign and domestic affairs. His most significant act as President paved the way for the annexation of Texas. Just a few days before he left office, Congress approved the measure, which offered Texas the opportunity to join the Union.

When Tyler's term was over, he went back to Virginia. In late 1861, as the Civil war was beginning, he was elected to the Confederate Congress. He died, however, in January 1842, while awaiting the convening of the Confederate Congress.

In Sherwood, Charles City County, Virginia, John Tyler dug a grave for his horse, "The General," above which he placed the following headstone: "Here lies the body of my good horse, 'The General.' For twenty years he bore me around the circuit of my practice, and in all that time he never made a blunder. Would that his master could say the same!"

JAMES K. POLK
11th President of the United States, 1845-1849
"Young Hickory"

Born: November 2, 1795, Mecklenburg County, NC
Died: June 15, 1849, Nashville, TN

James K. Polk was born in a log farmhouse outside of Charlotte, North Carolina in 1795. When he was 11 years old, his family moved near Columbia, Tennessee, where his father became a successful farmer.

After graduating with top honors from the University of North Carolina, Polk studied law, and in 1820 he was admitted to the bar and began practicing in Columbia. He was elected to the State legislature three years later.

In 1824 he married Sarah Childress; they were to have no children. Polk was elected to the U.S. House of Representatives in 1825, and from 1835 to 1839 he was Speaker of the House. In 1839, Polk quit Congress to run for Governor of Tennessee. He was elected, but in 1841 he was defeated in a bid for a second term. In 1843 he was defeated again.

The following year, Polk, running as the nation's first "dark horse" candidate, defeated Henry Clay and was elected President. A key to his victory was his expansionist platform, which demanded the annexation of Texas, the acquisition of

California, and the "reoccupation" of the Oregon Territory ("54-40 or Fight"). At 49 years of age, Polk was the youngest President ever to hold office.

In order to gain control of California, Polk sent the army to defend the United States' claim that Texas went all the way to the Rio Grande. The Mexican government was forced to fight, and the war turned out to be longer and bloodier than Polk ever expected. When Mexico finally surrendered, they signed the Treaty of Guadalupe Hidalgo (1848), by which Mexico surrendered the bulk of the present U.S. Southwest and recognized the Rio Grande as the boundary of Texas.

In the Northwest, Polk avoided war with the British by agreeing to a northern U.S. boundary line at the 49th parallel. Thus, in a brief span of time, Polk completed the acquisition of the majority of the present contiguous 48 states.

Along with Polk's territorial accomplishments were such domestic achievements as the reduction of tariffs, the reorganization of the Treasury, and the establishment of the U.S. Naval Academy and Smithsonian Institute.

President Polk refused to run for a second term. He retired to Nashville, Tennessee, and died a few months later.

ZACHARY TAYLOR
12th President of the United States, 1849-1850
"Old Rough and Ready"

Born: November 24, 1784, Orange County, VA
Died: July 9, 1850, Washington, D.C.

Zachary Taylor was raised in the small frontier village of Louisville, Kentucky. In his late teens, Taylor joined the Kentucky militia, and in 1808 entered the regular Army, serving as an infantry lieutenant at New Orleans. In 1810, he married Margaret Mackall Smith. Two of their six children died as children and one daughter went on to marry Jefferson Davis.

Taylor fought in William Henry Harrison's campaigns against the Indians, and later served as a major during the War of 1812. In 1832 he fought against Chief Black Hawk and was made a colonel. During the Seminole War, Tyler moved up to the rank of general.

In 1845, President James Polk sent General Taylor and his army to the Rio Grande, precipitating the Mexican War. During the Battle of Buena Vista he defeated a Mexican army four times larger than his own. He returned home to a hero's welcome and became the first President who had not served in the United States Congress or the Continental Congress.

In 1850, Taylor fell ill at the White House on Independence Day, shortly after attending a ceremony at the Washington Monument. He died a few days later at the age of 65.

MILLARD FILLMORE
13th President of the United States, 1850-1853
"The last Whig President"

Born: January 7, 1800, Locke, NY
Died: March 8, 1874, Buffalo, NY

Millard Fillmore was born into a humble family in 1800 at Cayuga County, in the Finger Lakes region on the central New York frontier, shortly after his parents had relocated there from Vermont. At 18 years of age the disadvantaged youth was a tall, good-looking boy, out of place among the seven and eight-year-olds with whom he shared the same school room. His teacher was a beautiful red-haired girl named Abigail Powers. She was so good at tutoring Millard, that when he turned 20 he was able to earn a job as a teacher himself in Buffalo, New York. It was at this point that Fillmore began studying law. In 1823 he was admitted to the bar. Three years later he married Abigail; they subsequently had a son and a daughter.

Fillmore quickly became a success. He entered the State Legislature in 1829. During the years 1833-35 and 1837-43 he sat in the U.S. House of Representatives, and eventually chaired the influential Ways and Means Committee.

In 1844, Fillmore unsuccessfully sought his party's nomination for Vice President and was narrowly defeated in a run for the governorship of New York. In 1844 he was elected as Vice President under Taylor.

In his new office, Fillmore presided over one of the most important debates in American history. Would the new Western territories be admitted as free states or slave states? The Senators from the South wanted slavery, while most of the Senators from the North wanted the territories to be free. Some Southerners began to talk about seceding from the Union.

Senator Henry Clay, from Kentucky, offered a compromise, later known as the Compromise of 1850. Passed in September 1850, the bill admitted California as a free state; founded the Utah and New Mexico Territories, whose residents were to choose whether or not slavery would prevail in their State constitutions; abolished the slave trade (but not slavery) in the District of Columbia; and created a tough Federal fugitive slave law known as the Fugitive Slave Act. This latter piece of legislation allowed a slave owner to follow his runaway slave into a free state and recapture him, while making it against the law to help a slave escape.

After Zachary Taylor's sudden death, Fillmore became President. In 1852 he dispatched Commodore Matthew C. Perry to Japan to establish trade and diplomatic relations. Fillmore lost the election of 1852. He died in 1874, at the age of 74.

FRANKLIN PIERCE
14th President of the United States, 1853-1857
"First President Born in the 19th Century"

Born: November 23, 1804, Hillsboro, NH
Died: October 8, 1869, Concord, NH

Franklin Pierce was born into a well-known New England family. His father, a farmer, tavern-keeper, and militia leader, went on to become Governor of New Hampshire. In 1824, Pierce graduated from Bowdoin College, Brunswick, Maine.

Pierce won admission to the bar in 1827, and two years later, at the age of 24, he was elected to the State Legislature (1829-33), where he eventually rose to the position of Speaker. In 1834, Pierce married Jane Means Appleton, the pretty daughter of the president of Bowdoin College. They were to have three sons, none of whom reached adulthood. Next came the stints in the U.S. House of Representatives (1833-37) and the Senate (1837-42), where he was the youngest member.

Pierce resigned from the Senate in 1842. He returned to his law practice, and later served as Federal District Attorney for New Hampshire (1845-46). When the Mexican War (1846-48) began, Pierce enlisted as a private. However, President Polk promptly made him a colonel, then a general under General Winfield Scott, although he had no military experience.

In 1852 Pierce, at the youthful age of 48, won the Presidential nomination. However, tragedy marred his election triumph when Pierce, his wife, and their last surviving child, an 11-year old son, were in a train wreck and the youngster perished before his parents' eyes. Pierce thus entered office in mourning, and his wife was unable to attend the inauguration.

The Kansas-Nebraska Act (1854), which Pierce supported, divided the unsettled central portion of the Louisiana Purchase into Kansas and Nebraska Territories. One goal of the legislation was to aid the construction of a transcontinental railroad. In order to appease the Southern Democrats, a provision that the settlers in the new Territories should decide their position on slavery for themselves was added.

Pierce supported and signed the bill, hoping that, if Kansas were admitted as a slave state and Nebraska as a free state, both sides would be mollified. But pro- and anti-slavery settlers poured into Kansas intending to influence the outcome of the vote. Sporadic guerrilla warfare — during which John Brown gained fame — broke out between the two factions. It proved to be a prelude to the Civil War.

Pierce died at Concord in 1869 at the age of 64.

JAMES BUCHANAN
15th President of the United States, 1857-1861
"The only President never to marry"

Born: April 23, 1791, Mercersburg, PA
Died: June 1, 1868, Lancaster, PA

James Buchanan's father owned a small country store just outside of Mercersburg, Pennsylvania, near the Maryland border. Young James learned to add and subtract and keep books by clerking in his father's modestly successful store. He was over six feet tall, broad-shouldered, and dignified

Buchanan attended Dickinson college, in Carlisle, Pennsylvania and graduated in 1809. He then studied law at Lancaster, where he was to maintain his home for the rest of his life. In 1812 he was admitted to the bar, thus beginning a highly successful legal career.

In 1814, the 23 year old Buchanan entered the lower house of the Pennsylvania legislature (1814-16), after which he resumed his law practice. In the summer of 1819, Buchanan was engaged to 23 year old Ann Caroline Coleman. While visiting Philadelphia, she took an overdose of laudanum and died there on December 9, 1819.

At the age of 30 Buchanan won a seat in the U.S. House of Representatives (1821-31). He was appointed Minister to Russia (1832-33), and then began a long stint in the U.S. Senate (1834-45), which included duty as chairman of the Foreign Relations Committee.

In 1844 he lost the Presidential nomination to James K. Polk. President Polk subsequently appointed Buchanan as his Secretary of State (1845-49), where he handled the negotiations which preceded and ended the Mexican War (1846-48). Buchanan also settled the Oregon question with Britain in 1846.

In 1856, Buchanan won the Presidential election. He was in office for only two days when the U.S. Supreme Court handed down the Dred Scott decision, which stated that slavery was legal in all United States territories not yet made into states. Still, Buchanan was unable to stop the factionalism that was destroying the Nation.

During his remaining months in office, Buchanan at first attempted to compromise with the secessionists. Early in 1861, however, the "lame-duck" President began taking stronger measures against the secessionists. He sent reinforcements and supplies in the unarmed merchant ship *Star of the West* to the besieged garrison at Fort Sumpter, South Carolina. When South Carolina batteries drove the ship away, Buchanan refused to evacuate the fort, but made no other attempt to resupply it. While the outbreak of war was averted, it proved to be only temporary. During his retirement, the tragedy of the Civil War affected him deeply. He died in 1868 at the age of 77.

ABRAHAM LINCOLN
16th President of the United States, 1861-1865
"Honest Abe"

Born: February 12, 1809, Hardin County, KY
Died: April 15, 1865, Washington, D.C.

Abraham Lincoln's father was a humble but ambitious farmer and carpenter. In 1816, when Abraham was 7 years old, the family moved to Indiana and settled near what is now Gentryville. Abraham helped build the cabin they lived in. It had only three walls, and on the open side a fire had to be kept going day and night. Two years later, Abraham's mother died during an epidemic. The following year, Abraham's father traveled to Elizabethtown, Kentucky, where he married a widow with three children, and returned to Indiana. Abraham's stepmother treated him and his sister Sarah kindly.

By now, Lincoln was six feet four inches tall, awkward, and homely looking. His coarse black hair stood up on his head, and outdoor work had made his arms and shoulders extremely strong. Lincoln's high-pitched voice sounded strange coming from such a tall, well-built body, but it never hampered his great ability to tell stories that made people laugh and laugh. Determined to avoid the hardships of frontier life in the future, Lincoln read as many books as he could find time for after he had finished the farm chores or his work as a handyman.

In 1831 the 22 year old Lincoln left home. He made a boat trip to New Orleans, and later in the year took positions as a clerk in a general store and millhand at New Salem, Illinois, all the while continuing to read voraciously and study law. In 1833-36, Lincoln served as postmaster of New Salem, and in 1834-36, after studying the subject at night, he performed surveying jobs in the area.

After being admitted to the bar, Lincoln won a seat in the State Legislature in 1834. He served until 1841, eventually taking over leadership of his party. In 1842, he married socially prominent Mary Todd of Lexington, Kentucky. They were to have four sons, only one of whom, Robert Todd, reached maturity. In 1846, Linclon was elected to the U.S. House of Representatives.

During his unsuccessful campaign for the Senate seat of incumbent Stephen A. Douglas in 1858, Lincoln gained nationwide fame in a series of debates around the state. Denouncing Illinois Democratic Senator Douglas' belief in popular sovereignty as the answer to the extension of slavery into the Territories, Lincoln emerged as a spokesman for moderate Republicans.

Lincoln won the Presidential election of 1860, but he was not to take office until March of 1861. In the meantime, one Southern state after another — convinced that Lincoln would destroy them both economically and politically — had begun seceding.

On April 12, 1861, Southern soldiers fired on the Union-held Fort Sumter in Charleston, South Carolina, thus launching the Civil War.

On September 22, 1862, President Lincoln issued his Emancipation Proclamation, which declared that all slaves in any state still in rebellion would be free. While the Emancipation Proclamation did not actually free the slaves — rather, it applied only to the rebellious states where Lincoln had no power to enforce it — it nevertheless won sympathy for the Union abroad and strengthened Northern morale. By the fall of 1864 it was clear the North was winning the war; Lincoln was easily elected to a second term later that year.

On April 9, 1865, General Robert E. Lee surrendered to Lincoln's general, Ulysses S. Grant, in the small village of Appomattox Courthouse, Virginia. Five days later, on the night of April 14, President and Mrs. Lincoln went to see a play at a Washington theater. During the performance, an actor named John Wilkes Booth stepped into the box behind Lincoln and shot him in the back of the head. The following day, one of the greatest men in all American history lay dead.

ANDREW JOHNSON
17th President of the United States, 1865-1869
"The only President ever to be impeached"

Born: December 29, 1808, Raleigh, NC
Died: July 31, 1875, Carter Station, TN

Andrew Johnson's father worked as a janitor, porter, and laborer in a Raleigh, North Carolina tavern. Andrew's mother was a maid in the same tavern. When Andrew was three years old, his father died in an accident and his mother had to take in washing to help feed her children. As a result, Andrew Johnson never attended school or received any formal education, though he did learn to read.

In 1822, his mother apprenticed the 13 year old Andrew and his brother to a tailor, whom the young boys grew to hate. Two years later, they both ran away from their master, first to Carthage, North Carolina, and then to Laurens, South Carolina, where they ran tailor shops.

The following year, Johnson returned to Greeneville and opened his own shop. By now, Johnson was a stocky young man who rarely laughed, but who had a great drive to get ahead in the world. When he was 18 years old, Johnson married Eliza McCardle who, though two years his junior, tutored him in reading and writing. Together, they would have three sons and two daughters.

After achieving modest prosperity in business, Johnson was elected to the town council before he was 21 years old. He then held the positions of Alderman (1828-30), Mayor (1830-33), State Legislator (1835-37 and 1839-41), State Senator (1841-43), U.S. Representative (1843-53), Governor of Tennessee (1853-57), and U.S. Senator (1857-62).

Because of Jonhson's Southern ties, secession created an enormous dilemma for him. He had been born and raised in the South, and he owned eight household slaves. He accepted the existence of slavery, insisting it was a unique institution beyond the control of Congress. But, believing secession to be unconstitutional, he chose to fight for the preservation of the Union.

Shortly after Lincoln's inauguration, in a desperate attempt at preventing his state from seceding, Johnson traveled to his home from Washington, D.C. to plead his case — despite threats to his life. En route, in Virginia, he was almost killed by a lynch mob. Faced with the increasing probability of death and possible capture by Confederate troops following the outbreak of war, Johnson finally returned to Washington, D.C. via Kentucky. Following Tennessee' secession in June of 1861, he was the only Senator from the South who remained in his chair, bringing him cheers from the North and scorn in the South.

In 1862, after Union forces captured Nashville, President Lincoln appointed Johnson as Military Governor of the State. Two years later, Johnson was nominated as Lincoln's running mate.

Upon being told that he, a former tailor, had been nominated on the same ticket with Abraham Lincoln, a former rail splitter, Johnson reportedly said, "What will the aristocrats do?"

When Lincoln was assassinated in April 1865, Johnson took over a task almost as difficult as the conduct of the war: reconstruction of the South. He adopted what he believed would have been Lincoln's moderate program, which had as its key the faith in the people of the South. Like Lincoln, Johnson — the first President without a military or legal background — did not want to take revenge on the Southern states. Instead, he wanted them brought back into the Union as quickly and easily as possible. While a few of the former leaders of the Confederacy were not pardoned, Johnson gave a pardon to any Southerner who would promise loyalty to the Union.

At Johnson's request, Congress began to discuss the ratification of the 13th amendment, which abolished slavery, as well as the addition of the 14th and 15th amendments to the Constitution. These amendments made former slaves citizens, and gave them the right to vote.

Congress then divided the South into five military districts, and the Federal Army was sent in to take command. Southern government officials were thrown out of office and new elections were held under military control.

However, as time went on a conflict between the President and the Congress began to grow in intensity. Radicals in Congress wanted stronger measures to be taken against the South. Johnson continued to veto such legislation, usually because he felt the rights of the States were being violated.

Finally, when Johnson tried to dismiss Secretary of War Edwin M. Stanton, a radical himself, Congress impeached Johnson, presumably because of his alleged violation of the Tenure of Office Act. With anger overruling reason — the real issue, after all, was whether Congress or the President would direct Reconstruction — the Senate tried him in the spring of 1868. Out of 54 senators, 36 voted to impeach Johnson, while 19 voted to acquit him. However, the law required a two-thirds majority in order for impeachment to take place. Thus, Johnson was acquitted by only one lone vote. After the trial, the Radicals continued their strong legislative efforts, but were never able to secure either equal rights for blacks or Republican control of the South. Johnson fought off the Radicals throughout the remainder of his Presidency, but his power and reputation had been severely damaged.

Johnson's term ended soon after his impeachment hearing. Often overlooked from his administration was the 1867 purchase of Alaska from Russia by Secretary of State William H. Seward. While many people initially referred to this acquisition as "Seward's folly," the fact is that for the sum of $7,200,000, the United States gained control of a vast territory that was rich in natural resources.

After leaving office, Johnson retired to Tennessee. Six years later he was once more elected to the U.S. Senate, where Senators who had once voted against him stood and applauded when he entered for the first time. He was the first President to become a Senator after his term had ended. But, after serving for only a few months, he died at the age of 66 while visiting the rural home of one of his daughters, about 40 miles from Greeneville.

ULYSSES S. GRANT
18th President of the United States, 1869-1877
"Unconditional Surrender" Grant

Born: April 27, 1822, Point Pleasant, OH
Died: July 23, 1885, Mount McGregor, NY

Hiram Ulysses Grant was born in 1822 along the banks of the Ohio River. His father was a farmer and a tanner who had immigrated from Kentucky. The year after Ulysses' birth, the family moved to nearby Georgetown.

After a rather average childhood and young adulthood, the 27 year old Grant received an appointment to the United States Military Academy, which he reluctantly entered. Because of an error — the Congressman who appointed him to the military academy thought his first two names were Ulysses Simpson; Simpson was his mother's maiden name — he was registered as Ulysses Simpson Grant.

As a young lieutenant, Grant served under General Zachary Taylor and General Winfield Scott in the Mexican War (1846-48). In 1848, Grant married Juia Dent, the sister of an Academy classmate, who was to bear three sons and one daughter. But when he was ordered to military duty in the West, Grant was not allowed to take his family with him. Lonely, he began to drink, a problem that became so serious his commanding officer told him he had to either quit drinking or resign. Grant chose to resign.

Upon his return, his father-in-law gave him a small farm near St. Louis. While Grant enjoyed the work, the land was poor and he couldn't earn a decent living. He moved his family to St. Louis and tried his hand at real estate, only to encounter failure once again. Unsuccessful jobs selling firewood and collecting bills followed, until finally his brothers gave him a job in a tannery/leather store they owned in Galena, Illinois. The 39 year old Grant was still drinking too much, his salary was a meager 50 dollars a month, and his family and friends considered him a failure.

In one of the most dramatic personal turn-arounds in history, three years later, in 1864, Grant was a Lieutenant General in command of all the U.S. armies, In 1868 he was elected President of the United States. He served two terms, and seven years after he left office he was unemployed and desperate for money once again.

It all began with the outset of the Civil War in 1861, when the North desperately needed trained officers. Grant was appointed a colonel in the army and quickly rose to the rank of General. Grant first gained fame during his campaigns in the Mississippi River Valley, culminating in his capture of Vicksburg, Mississippi, which split the

Confederacy. In March 1864, after Grant's victory at Chattanooga, President Lincoln placed him in command of the Union Armies.

Grant's impressive victories brought an end to the Civil War and made him a national hero. He was mobbed by crowds of people wherever he went. In 1865, he narrowly escaped possible assassination at Ford's Theatre only because he and his wife declined the President's invitation to attend the performance. While he had never been interested in politics — he had only voted fo President once in his life — the Republicans nominated him for President in 1868. He won the election by a wide margin.

Grant was well trained to be a general, but ill prepared for the Presidency. Leaving the South to Congress, one harsh law after another was passed against that portion of the country. While he helped set up Yellowstone National Park, the first national park in the country, he had no legislative program to speak of. Grant also naively introduced friends and wealthy men into his Cabinet and staff, many of whom turned out to be highly corrupt. As a result, though Grant himself was an honest man, several scandals rocked his administration, including the Credit Mobilier and the Whiskey Ring. Laws passed by Congress and enforced by federal troops ended up establishing crooked state governments in the South. Meanwhile, in the North, railroads and whiskey manufacturers were notorious for bribing government officials.

When his second term ended, the still-popular Grant went on a trip around the world. During these two-plus years, he and his family enjoyed royal treatment and met dozens of world leaders.

Upon his return to New York he bought a large house. Needing money to continue this lavish lifestyle, he invested everything he had in a banking business, leaving the management of his affairs to "friends." The business promptly went bankrupt and Grant suddenly found himself deeply in debt.

Penniless and humiliated, Grant — who smoked some 20 cigars a day — was stricken with cancer of the throat. Refusing to accept charity, he signed an offer from a publisher to write his memoirs. In spite of the tremendous pain he was suffering, Grant finished his autobiography just four days before his death in 1885 in the summer cottage of a friend at Mount McGregor, New York. The book became a classic and went on to earn his heirs nearly half a million dollars in royalties.

RUTHERFORD B. HAYES
19th President of the United States, 1877-1881
"First President in office to visit the West Coast"

Born: October 4, 1822, Delaware, OH
Died: January 17, 1893, Fremont, OH

Rutherford Hayes' father, a storekeeper and farmer, died before his son's birth at Delaware, Ohio, in 1822. In 1842, at the age of 20, Hayes graduated at the top of his class from Kenyon College, Ohio. He then studied law for a year at Columbus, and in 1845 completed Harvard Law School. He subsequently took up practice at Lower Sandusky (now Fremont), Ohio.

In 1849 Hayes moved to Cincinnati, where he gained fame as a criminal lawyer and defender of fugitive slaves. In 1852 he married Lucy Ware Webb, who would later become the first wife of a President to be a college graduate. Together, they were to have seven sons and a daughter.

When the Civil War began, Hayes was appointed as a major in the Ohio Volunteer Infantry. He was wounded four times and had four horses killed from under him, and before the war was over he had risen to the rank of brevet major general.

Hayes was still in the Army when, in 1864, he was elected to the U.S. House of Representatives (1865-67). He resigned in the latter year to run for Governor of Ohio. While in office he helped

61

blacks obtain the right to vote and was instrumental in the formation of Ohio State University.

During the Presidential nomination in 1876, Hayes went to bed on election night believing he had been defeated by Democrat Samuel J. Tilden, Governor of New York. However, an unprecedented and intricate election dispute followed, and for months the Government and the country were in a quandary. The complication arose from the fact that a few states had submitted two different sets of electoral votes. Tilden needed to win only one of the disputed votes; Hayes needed to win all of them. The issue was resolved by a special Congressional commission only 2 days before the inauguration. In order to prevent a Democratic filibuster from holding up the proceedings, the Republicans promised Southern Democrats that the role of Federal troops in Reconstruction would end. On April 24, 1877, Hayes kept the promise, and the last federal troops left Louisiana. The long bloody period known as the Reconstruction Era was over.

On the whole, Hayes left the government more honest than he had originally found it. He refused to run for a second term and returned to his home in Ohio, where he died on January 17, 1893.

JAMES A. GARFIELD
20th President of the United States, 1881
"The first left-handed President"

Born: November 19, 1831, Orange, OH
Died: September 19, 1881, Elberon, NJ

James Garfield was born in 1831 at Orange Township in Cuyahoga County, Ohio. His father, a canal worker turned farmer, died before James was 2 years old, and the boy was raised by his mother and older brother. They were extremely poor and James had little chance to go to school. Instead, as a teenager he drove boat teams on the Ohio and Erie Canal, while dreaming of a life at sea.

However, Garfield then decided that he wanted an education. He began to attend classes wherever and whenever he could. A quick learner, Garfield was soon able to write Latin with one hand and Greek with the other at the same time. After graduating from Williams College, in Williamstown, Massachusetts, Garfeld joined the faculty at Western Reserve Eclectic Institute (Hiram College after 1867) at Hiram, Ohio. In 1857, he became president of the Institute, and the following year he married childhood friend Lucretia Rudolph, who was to bear five sons and two daughters.

In 1859, Garfield was elected to the State Senate (1860-61). He also studied enough law to be admitted to the bar, setting up practice in Hiram.

With the outbreak of the war in 1861, Garfield was commissioned in the Ohio Volunteer Infantry. The next year he was made the youngest brigadier general in the Army.

In late 1863 Garfield reluctantly resigned from the Army to take a seat in the U.S. House of Representatives. The Congressman was to serve for the next 18 years until 1880, when the Republican-controlled Ohio legislature elected Garfield to the U.S. Senate. However, Garfield never served as a Senator, because he soon won his party's Presidential nomination. After the convention became hopelessly deadlocked over three candidates, Garfield proved to be victorious as a "dark horse" on the 36th ballot.

On July 2, 1881, when a vacation-bound Garfield arrived at Washington's Baltimore and Potomac Railroad Station, Charles Julius Guiteau, a disappointed office-seeker who had wanted to be appointed United States consul at Paris shot the President twice in the back.

Undergoing numerous medical treatments, including Alexander Graham Bell's attempts to find the bullet with his newly invented induction balance electrical device, Garfield lingered on for 80 days. On September 6, 1881, the President was taken to the seaside resort of Elberon, New Jersey, to recuperate, but he died there of blood poisoning on September 19, 1881. Guiteau was hanged in Washington, D.C., on June 30, 1882.

CHESTER ALAN ARTHUR
21st President of the United States, 1881-1885
"The Gentleman Boss"

Born: October 5, 1829, Fairfield, VT
Died: November 18, 1886, New York, NY

Chester Alan Arthur was the eldest son in a large family fathered by a Baptist minister who had immigrated from Ireland via Canada. Chester was born in 1830 near the Canadian border at Fairfield, Vermont. When he was 14 years old, his family relocated to Schenectady, New York.

Arthur studied at the Lyceum School for a year and then at Union College, where he graduated with honors in 1848. Over the next several years, Arthur taught school in Vermont, eventually ascending to the rank of principal. In his spare time he studied law, and was admitted to the bar in 1853. That same year he joined a New York City firm managed by family friends.

In 1859, Arthur married Ellen Lewis Herndon of Fredricksburg, Virginia, the daughter of a well-known naval officer. Together they would raise one daughter and two sons.

Arthur's interest in politics led to jobs with political "bosses," men who tried to control elections by giving jobs and money to people who would vote the way they wanted. Over time, Arthur, a friendly, good-humored man, became an important political boss himself.

In 1871, President Grant, in what was essentially a reward for his party loyalty, appointed Arthur as Collector of Customs of the Port of New York. In this position, Arthur went along with the so-called "spoils system," hiring more personnel than were needed, and expecting them to support the party — in particular U.S. Senator Roscoe Conkling.

When Rutherford B. Hayes became President, he brought to the office the belief that government officials should not take part in the management of political parties. The ever-loyal Arthur refused to obey, and as a result, Hayes forced him out of his job.

Arthur went back to his law practice, and eventually received the Vice Presidential nomination under James Garfield. When Garfield was assassinated in 1881, Arthur took over the Presidency. To the shock and dismay of Conkling and his followers, Arthur set about rehabilitating the civil service. Rising above partisanship, he abandoned his party loyalties and became an ardent reformer.

Garfield helped bring the Navy up to date with modern ships, signed a bill creating a rudimentary government in Alaska, and changed the postal system so that they were able to give better and cheaper service. At the close of his term,

Arthur marked the beginning of the electrical age when he pressed a button at the White House that set machinery in motion at a New Orleans exhibition. In February 1885 he dedicated the Washington Monument.

While Arthur was a respected and popular President, he had made too many enemies within his own party. In 1884 he lost his party's nomination for the U.S. Senate from New York. Arthur retired to New York City and died less than 2 years later.

GROVER CLEVELAND
22nd President of the United States, 1885-1889
24th President of the United States, 1893-1897
"Only President to serve nonconsecutive terms"

Born: March 18, 1837, Caldwell, NJ
Died: June 24, 1908, Princeton, NJ

Grover Cleveland's father was a Presbyterian pastor who had many children but very little money. When Grover was 14 he had to quit school and go work in a store, and when his father died a few years later, the young man headed for Cleveland, Ohio — apparently because he liked the name of the city — in search of better economic opportunity.

However, Cleveland only made it to his uncle's stock farm in Buffalo, New York, where he got a job in a lawyer's office making four dollars a week. The job gave him the chance to study, and by the time he was 22, he was admitted to the bar.

During the mid-1870s, Cleveland attained recognition as one of the leading lawyers in the Western part of the State. In 1881 he was asked by the Democratic party to run for mayor of Buffalo. Once elected, he launched attacks on machine politics that irritated even his own party. Cleveland reorganized the city so that it ran more cheaply, fired anybody he caught stealing or taking bribes, and within a year had cleaned up the town. His impressive record helped him win the Democratic gubernatorial nomination in 1882.

In 1884, Cleveland was nominated by the Democrats to run for President.Once elected, Cleveland began to reform the federal government just as he had the state government of New York. He opened thousands of acres of land to homesteaders that the railroads had illegally claimed had been granted to them, he improved the civil service by getting better government workers, he returned almost 500,000 acres of reservation to the Indians, and he made sure the Navy received the best ships for the least amount of money possible.

In 1886, Cleveland married 21-year-old Frances Folsom, the daughter of a former law partner who, upon his death, had left her as Cleveland's ward. It was the only Presidential wedding ever held in the White House, and Mrs Cleveland was the youngest of all First Ladies. Together, the couple would have two sons and three daughters.

In 1889, despite capturing the plurality of the popular vote, Cleveland lost the election to Republican Benjamin Harrison. When Mrs. Cleveland moved out of the White House, she reportedly told the servants to take good care of it. "I want everything just the way it is now when we come back," she had said. "That will be exactly four years from now."

She was right, because after spending 4 years practicing law in New York, Cleveland was easily reelected over Harrison in the election of 1892. He thus became the only President in U.S. history to serve two terms that did not directly follow each other.

Upon entering office, the panic of 1893 hit the country. Companies went bankrupt, banks failed, mortgages were foreclosed, and unemployment rose drastically. In 1895, Cleveland strengthened the gold standard and bolstered Treasury reserves by obtaining a loan from Wall Street tycoons J.P. Morgan and August Belmont.

A conservationist, Cleveland signed the Yellowstone Act, which was the first Federal legislation designed to protect wildlife on Government lands. Three years later, in 1897, he set aside some 21 million acres of forest reserves.

Because Cleveland's conservative economic policies failed to end the depression, the Republicans won landslide victories in the congressional elections of 1894. Two years later, Cleveland failed to win his party's nomination.

After an active retirement spent in Princeton, New Jersey, where he sat on the board of trustees of the universiity, Cleveland passed away in 1908.

BENJAMIN HARRISON
23rd President of the United States, 1889-1893
"Little Ben"

Born: August 20, 1833, North Bend, OH
Died: March 13, 1901, Indianapolis, IN

Benjamin Harrison was born in 1833 at North Bend, Ohio, on the estate of his grandfather, William Henry Harrison, who was to become President seven years later. In 1852, Harrison graduated from Miami University, at Oxford, Ohio. The following year, he married Caroline L. Scott, who later gave birth to a son and a daughter.

After studying law with a prestigious Cincinnati firm from 1852 until 1854, Harrison, a small man at five feet six inches tall, was admitted to the bar. In 1854 he moved to Indianapolis, where he established a practice. Within two years he was one of the city's top attorneys.

When the national railroad strike hit the country in 1877, Harrison was appointed to the Indianapolis strike settlement committee. The following year he chaired the Republican State convention, and in 1880 he led the delegation to the national convention, where he played a significant role in nominating James A. Garfield. Refusing to accept a Cabinet post, Harrison instead took a seat in the U.S. Senate (1881-87).

His election came fairly easily, partially because

his name was so well known — his father had been a Congressman and his grandfather, William Henry Harrison, had been President.

In 1888 the Republicans nominated Harrison for President. In a very close race Harrison gained the majority of electoral votes despite losing the popular vote to Grover Cleveland, and was elected to the office of the Chief Executive.

Under his administration, Congress passed the controversial McKinley Tarriff Act, which placed a high tax on goods shipped to the United States from other countries. In 1889 Harrison opened the Oklahoma District to homesteaders. The following year he approved legislation which created several national parks, and in 1891 he set aside more than 13 million acres of public land for national forest preserves. During Harrison's admistration, a record number of six States — North and South Dakota, Montana, Washington, Idaho, and Wyoming — were admitted to the Union.

Largely because of the unpopular McKinley Tariff, Harrison was defeated for reelection in 1892. He returned to his home in Indianapolis as a widower — two weeks before the election, his wife had died. In retirement, Harrison resumed his law practice and continued to write books about United States government. In 1896 he married widow Mary Scott Lord Dimmick, a niece of his first wife. Together they were to have one daughter. Harrison passed away in 1901.

WILLIAM MCKINLEY
25th President of the United States, 1897-1901
"The third Chief Executive to be assassinated"

Born: January 29, 1843, Niles, OH
Died: September 14, 1901, Buffalo, NY

William McKinley was born in the small town of Niles, Ohio, in 1843. In 1852, his father, an iron-maker, moved to another tiny village, nearby Poland. In 1860 he enrolled at Allegheny College, in Meadvile, Pennsylvania, but illness and his family's financial problems forced him to drop out after only one term.

In 1861, McKinley, a pale, dignified man, enlisted in an Ohio infantry regiment commanded by Colonel and future-President Rutherford B. Hayes. By the time the war ended, McKinley had achieved the rank of brevet major. When he returned to Ohio, McKinley studied law, and in the fall of 1866 he entered Albany (N.Y.) Law School. He later established a practice in Canton.

After campaigning for his army friend Hayes, McKinley won election as prosecuting attorney of Stark County (1869-71). In the latter year, he married Ida Saxtoin, the daughter of a local banker. Following the early deaths of their two daughters, Ida, who suffered from epilepsy after 1873, became semi-invalid and remained so for the rest of her life.

From 1877 to 1891, McKinley served as a Congressman, becoming one of the leaders of the Republican party. In 1891 he was elected Governor of Ohio, and in 1892 he chaired the Republican national convention.

McKinley was elected President in 1896.

Meanwhile, in 1895 Cuba had renewed its revolt against Spain. Publicizing the many incidents of Spanish repression, the American "yellow press" encouraged public sentiment for intervention. And when the U.S. battleship *Maine* mysteriously exploded while on a courtesy call to Havana, McKinley, who had kept the United States neutral during the early part of his term as President, bowed to public and Congressional pressure and on April 11, 1898, demanding independence for the island, asked Congress to declare war with Spain.

Soon after, acting Secretary of the Navy Theodore Roosevelt took matters into his own hands and sent ships to the Spanish-owned Philippine Islands. The American fleet quickly destroyed the Spanish fleet, thus helping to swiftly end the war in the Pacific. It took several months, however, for the War Department to gather enough American soldiers to send to Cuba. Nevertheless, 100 days after McKinley's declaration of war, the United States defeated Spain on that island. Under the terms of the Treaty of Paris, Cuba was declared independent and the United States took control of the Philippines as well as the islands of Guam and Puerto Rico.

At McKinley's request, Congress quickly voted to annex the Hawaiian islands, and on July 7, 1898, Hawaii became an American territory.

In 1900 McKinley was elected to a second term. The following year, on September 6, 1901, at the Pan-American Exposition in Buffalo, New York, McKinley was shaking hands with a huge crowd of admirers. He had just taken the flower he was wearing on his coat and given it to a little girl when a man with a handkerchief wrapped around his right hand approached him as if to shake hands. Inside of the handkerchief was a gun, and he fired two shots into the President. The man's name was Leon Czolgosz, an anarchist who said he longed to kill a great ruler. Eight days later McKinley died. Czolgosz was tried in the Supreme Court of New York and was convicted. He was electrocuted on October 29, 1901, at Auburn State Prison, Auburn, New York.

THEODORE ROOSEVELT
26th President of the United States, 1901-1909
"Speak softly and carry a big stick"

Born: October 27, 1858, New York, NY
Died: January 6, 1919, Long Island, NY

Theodore Roosevelt was born in 1858 in lower Manhattan to a successful glass importer, merchant, and banker-father, and a mother who came from an aristocratic Georgian bckground. As a child, Roosevelt suffered from an asthmatic condition, causing him to be frail and sickly looking. Deciding to overcome this condition, he began to build up his body through swimming and weight lifting. He slowly overcame his poor health, eventually developing a muscular chest, powerful arms and shoulders, and impressive endurance.

When he was 18 years old, Roosevelt entered Harvard University. He graduated Phi Beta Kappa four years later, a member of the boxing team. During his senior year, he began writing *The Naval War of 1812* (1882), which was the first of approximately 40 books and dozens of articles he was to publish in the fields of history, politics, and adventure over the course of his life.

Upon graduating, Roosevelt married Alice Hathaway Lee of Boston. In 1884, Roosevelt's wife and his mother both died within a few hours of each other.

In an attempt to forget his grief, Roosevelt moved to the Badlands of the Dakota Territory, where he bought a ranch and worked as a cowboy.

Two years later, Roosevelt returned to the East. After marrying again, he served in Washington on the Civil Service Commission and in New York City as commissioner of police. In 1897, President McKinley appointed him Assistant Secretary of the Navy.

When the Spanish-American War erupted, Roosevelt quit his government job and formed a cavalry regiment called the "Rough Riders." In perhaps the most famous battle in Cuba, Roosevelt led his contingent in a charge up San Juan Hill to capture a Spanish fort. After the war ended, Roosevelt, still riding high from his military triumphs, was elected Governor of New York. In 1900, he accepted the Vice Presidential nomination. When McKinley was assassinated, Roosevelt took over office — he was 42 years and 10 months old when sworn in, the youngest man ever to run the Nation.

Operating under the belief that the President was limited only by specific constitutional prohibitions, Roosevelt inaugurated his "Square Deal" reform program, which promised equitable treatment for labor, capital, and the general public. Nicknamed the "Trust Buster," Roosevelt initiated many law suits against trusts, and encouraged legislation to speed up prosecution. He forced the railroads to give fair rates to small businesses, insisted the owners of coal mines pay better wages, was instrumental in the enactment of the Pure Food and Drug Act (1906), and signed legislation for the inspection of stockyards and packinghouses.

In 1904, Roosevelt was reelected by a huge majority. During his second term in office, he established national parks and more than 125 million acres of national forests, founded many wildlife preserves, and set aside extensive coal reserves and land for potential public dam sites.

Roosevelt began construction of the Panama Canal (1904-1914) under the Army Corps of Engineers, and while inspecting the operation he became the first President to leave U.S. soil while in office. His role in negotiating the Treaty of Portsmouth (1905),which ended the Russo-Japanese War, earned him the Nobel Peace Prize (1906) — the first American to do so.

Roosevelt was also the first President to ride in an automobile, the first to fly in an airplane, and the first to submerge in a submarine.

Refusing to run for a third term, Roosevelt instead went big game hunting in Africa, toured Europe, wrote books, and made speeches. However, in 1912, Roosevelt, feeling that President Taft had abandoned his policies, sought the Presidential nomination. While campaigning in Milwaukee, Wisconsin, Roosevelt survived an attempt on his life. He was leaving the Hotel Gilpatrick, en route to the Auditorium to make a speech, when John Nepomuk Schrank, a saloon keeper, shot him in the chest.

Although the bullet tore through his coat and his shirt was covered with blood, Roosevelt said, "I will deliver this speech or die, one or the other." He spoke for approximately 50 minutes before going to the hospital. On November 13, 1912 Schrank, who claimed he was opposed to Roosevelt's desire to serve a third term, was declared insane and was committed.

Roosevelt, running on the Progressive, or "Bull Moose" ticket, lost the election to Democrat Woodrow Wilson when the Republican voters split between William Howard Taft and himself. In 1919, while some Republicans were once again discussing the possibility of his Presidential candidacy, Roosevelt died at the age of 61.

WILLIAM HOWARD TAFT
27th President of the United States, 1909-1913
"Big Bill"

Born: September 15, 1857, Cincinnati, OH
Died: March 8, 1930, Washington, D.C.

William Howard Taft's father was a wealthy lawyer and judge who served under President Grant as Secretary of War and Attorney General, and under President Arthur as Minister to Austria-Hungary and Russia. A good tennis player and an excellent dancer, Taft eventually grew to be about six feet tall, weighing in at close to 300 pounds.

In 1878, Taft graduated from Yale as the class salutatorian. After studying at Cincinnati Law School (1878-1880), he was admitted to the bar. In 1886 he married Helen Herron, the daughter of a leading State Republican, who was to bear two sons and one daughter.

In 1887, the Governor of Ohio appointed Taft to the State Supreme Court. The following year he ran for the office of judge and was elected. With the exception of the Presidency, this was the only election in which he would ever participate. From 1892-1900, Taft was Federal Judge for the Sixth Circuit (Ohio, Kentucky, Michigan, and Tennessee). While on the bench, he was also the Dean of the Cincinnati Law School (1896-1900).

In 1901 Taft was appointed Civil Governor of the Philippines. Over the next three years, he encouraged limited self-government; built roads, harbors, and schools; improved the court system; and reformed the economy.

In 1904 President Theodore Roosevelt appointed Taft Secretary of War, and it was largely because of Roosevelt that the Republican party nominated Taft for President in 1908. With Roosevelt's backing he was elected.

During his single term in office, Taft improved the civil service. He initiated more antitrust suits than Roosevelt, and was the first President to set aside government-owned lands where oil and coal had been found, claiming that the profit from these should belong to the people, not to private businesses. Arizona and New Mexico, the last of the 48 contiguous States, were admitted to the Union during his administration.

Taft was the first President to pitch a ball to open the professional baseball season. On April 14, 1910, he tossed the baseball before the American League game between Washington and Philadelphia. The crowd of 12,226 who had come to watch the proceedings broke all previous attendance records.

Upon leaving office, Taft, who had been one of the most unhappy Presidents ever elected, said: "I am glad to be going. This is the lonesomest place in the world." He returned to his legal career, and from 1913 until 1921, he held a chair in constitutional law at Yale University. Taft also served as an official in a variety of philanthropic and educational institutions, including the American Red Cross, and the Hampton Institute. In 1921, President Harding fulfilled Taft's life-long dream by appointing him as Chief Justice of the Supreme Court (1921-30). It was the first time a President had ever held such a post. This was the work he truly loved, and he served until ill health forced his retirement. In 1930, a month after resigning, he died in Washington, D.C.

WOODROW WILSON
28th President of the United States, 1913-1921
"Make the world safe for democracy"

Born: December 29, 1856, Staunton, VA
Died: February 3, 1924, Washington, D.C.

Thomas Woodrow Wilson was born in 1856 at the First Presbyterian Church in Staunton, Virginia, where his father was the pastor. In 1879, Wilson graduated from the College of New Jersey (now Princeton University). While at Princeton he had played football and later helped coach the team.

In 1882, Wilson received his law degree from the University of Virginia Law School, was admitted to the Georgia bar, and set up practice in Atlanta. A year later, after losing interest in the profession, he enrolled at the graduate school of Johns Hopkins University in Baltimore. In 1885, he married Ellen L. Axson, the daughter of a Presbyterian minister. Together, the couple had three daughters.

Wilson, who had a high forehead, a long, thin nose, and a firm mouth, looked like a teacher, and indeed, from 1885 until 1888 he held a professorship of history at Bryn Mawr (Pennsylvania) College. During this period, he earned his Ph.D. in political science from Johns Hopkins. By 1902 he had authored nine books and 32 articles, and that same year he was made president of Princeton University.

In 1910, Wilson was elected Governor of New Jersey, and two years later he won the Presidential election, becoming the first Chief Executive who had been president of a major university. Within two years and 170 days, he had risen from a citizen who had never been a candidate for a public office to President of the United States.

Through the Underwood Tariff (1913), Wilson got Congress to lower the rates and instituted the first constitutional Federal income tax. Wilson established the Federal Trade Commission (1914), strengthened antitrust legislation, recognized the rights of labor unions and their right to strike, and initiated regularly scheduled press conferences.

In the meantime, Wilson's wife died in 1914. The following year, he married widow Edith Bolling Galt. The couple had no children.

When World War I began in Europe, Wilson proclaimed U.S. neutrality. During the 1916 election campaign, his supporters used the slogan "He kept us out of the war." Wilson was elected to a second term by an extremely narrow margin.

In April 1917, after German U-boats continued to sink American vessels, Wilson finally asked Congress to declare war. Wilson claimed that this would be a "war to end all wars," and even while the fighting was going on he drew up his famous Fourteen Points peace plan. The most important portion of this plan called for a League of Nations, an impartial organization that would represent every country. It was Wilson's dream that such a league could settle all future arguments between nations. When Germany surrendered in November of 1918, provisions for the league were incorporated into the Treaty of Versailles. These efforts were to win Wilson the Nobel Peace Prize in 1919.

In October 1919 a stroke incapacitated Wilson, and he remained under the care of his wife until Harding took over the Presidency in March of 1921. He died in 1924.

WARREN G. HARDING
29th President of the United States, 1921-1923
"Return to normalcy"

Born: November 2, 1865, Corsica, OH
Died: August 2, 1923, San Francisco, CA

Warren G. Harding, a tall, handsome, and bright boy, was born in 1865 on a farm in Corsica, a rural town in north-central Ohio. After receiving his B.S. degree from Ohio Central College at Iberia (1879-82), Harding taught briefly in a country school, then earned a position on the *Democratic Mirror*, a weekly newspaper in Marion, Ohio. A year or so later he and two friends bought a bankrupt weekly paper called the *Star* for 300 dollars.

The town of Marion was booming, and the paper grew with it. In 1891 Harding married Florence Kling DeWolfe, the divorced daughter of a local banker. They were to have no children.

After an unsuccessful bid for the Governorship, Harding was elected to the State Senate (1899-1903), where he became floor leader, and then held the position of Lieutenant Governor (1904-06).Harding next served in the U.S. Senate (1915-21) where, in 1916, he chaired the Republican convention and delivered the keynote address.

During the 1920 Presidential election, Harding and running mate Calvin Coolidge won more than 60 percent of the popular vote. Harding assembled the Washington Conference (1921-22), during which five of the major powers in attendance — the United States, Great Britain, Japan, Italy, and France — signed several treaties, including the Five-Power Treaty, which set a ratio of warships, restricted their tonnage and armament, and limited the use of submarines. Another treaty eliminated the use of poison gas in warfare.

In August 1923, Harding became ill while visiting Alaska. A few days later he died in San Francisco. After his death, the Teapot Dome scandal reached the public. Albert B. Fall, the Secretary of the Interior, had rented publicly owned oil fields to private companies in exchange for over three million dollars in bribes. Fall was subsequently fined and sent to prison.

CALVIN COOLIDGE
30th President of the United States, 1923-1929
"The business of America is business"

Born: July 4, 1872, Plymouth Notch, VT
Died: January 5, 1933, Northampton, MA

John Calvin Coolidge, Jr. was born on Independence Day 1872 in Plymouth Notch, Vermont Coolidge graduated from Amherst College and after being admitted to the bar in 1897, practiced law in Northampton, Massachusetts.

With his lean, sour look — his mouth turned down at the corners — Coolidge gave people the impression of being safe, conservative, and totally honest. Nicknamed "Silent Cal," he held the city offices of councilman, solicitor, and court clerk from 1899-1904. The following year, he married Grace A. Goodhue, a teacher at the Northampton School for the Deaf. Together they were to raise two sons.

After serving as Mayor of Northampton, Coolidge was elected Lieutenant Governor in 1916, and Governor in 1918. In 1919 he was elected as President Harding's Vice President.

In 1923, Coolidge was visiting his father when he received the news that Harding had passed away. After being awakened by a messenger in the middle of the night and told that he was now

President, Coolidge took the oath of office from his father, a justice of the peace, next to the flickering light of a kerosene lamp, his hand resting on an old family Bible.

Coolidge was nominated for reelection in 1924, and pledged to continue "Coolidge prosperity." He chose not to run for reelection in 1928 and retired to Northampton the following year, only a few months before the Wall Street Crash and the start of the Great Depression. He died in 1933 at Northampton.

HERBERT HOOVER
31st President of the United States, 1929-1933
"First Chief Executive elected from California"

Born: August 10, 1874, West Branch, IA
Died: October 20, 1964, New York City, NY

Herbert Hoover, the first President from west of the Mississippi River, was born in 1874 at West Branch, Iowa. His father, a blacksmith and farm implement salesman, died six years later. His mother, a deeply religious Quaker, supported her three children by preaching and taking in sewing. She died when Herbert was nine.

In 1895, Hoover graduated from Stanford University with a degree in engineering. When he was 23 he went to Australia, where he helped develop one of the richest gold mines in the world. Two years later he returned to California and married his college sweetheart, Lou Henry, the daughter of a Monterey, California banker. The newlyweds set sail the following day, and for the next two decades they shared many adventures on several continents. While still in his 30s, Hoover became a multimillionaire.

At the outbreak of World War I in 1914, Hoover, who then was visiting England, voluntarily headed the American Relief Committee (1914-15), which offered aid to Americans who were stranded in Europe because of the war. Next, directing the

Commission for Relief in Belgium (1915-18), Hoover distributed food, clothing, and medicine to war-ravaged Belgian and French civilians, and arranged with Allied and German officials to distribute these supplies on both sides of the lines. Because of his great efforts, President Harding appointed Hoover Secretary of Commerce.

In 1928, after Collidge refused to seek renomination, the national convention nominated Hoover for President. In 1929, shortly after Hoover took office, the Wall Street stock market crashed, and the economy quickly collapsed. A proponent of individualism and self-reliance, Hoover felt that massive Federal aid would only serve to undermine the country's moral fiber. Instead, he championed the belief that relief for the impoverished should come from volunteer organizations and State and local governments. Despite taking measures to stimulate business recovery, the depression deepened, and many people began to hold Hoover personally responsible.

In 1932 Hoover was defeated by Democrat Franklin D. Roosevelt. During his long and active retirement, Hoover wrote extensively on history and politics, and completed his memoirs. Additionally, Hoover participated in several civic and charitable organizations, and received numerous awards, medals, and honorary degrees. He died in 1964 in New York City.

FRANKLIN D. ROOSEVELT
32nd President of the United States, 1933-1945
"The only thing we have to fear is fear itself."

Born: January 30, 1882, Hyde Park, NY
Died: April 12, 1945, Warm Springs, GA

Franklin Delano Roosevelt was born into a wealthy and well-known family in 1882 on a Hudson River estate at Hyde Park, New York. President Theodore Roosevelt was Franklin's fifth cousin, and he was also distantly related to ten other Presidents: Washington, John and John Quincy Adams, Madison, Van Buren, William and Benjamin Harrison, Taylor, Grant, and Taft.

As a child, Roosevelt never went to public schools, but was instead taught by his parents and private tutors. Frequent travel in Europe enabled him to learn the French and German languages. Roosevelt, a tall, lean, good-looking young man, earned a B.A. degree in history at Harvard in only 3 years (1900-03). He then studied law at New York City's Columbia University. While still in law school he married a distant cousin, Eleanor Roosevelt, who was to become the best known and most widely loved of all the First Ladies. Together they would raise one daughter and five sons. When Roosevelt passed the bar in 1907 after only three years of study, he quit school without taking a degree.

In 1913, after a stint in the New York State Legislature, President Wilson appointed Roosevelt Assistant Secretary of the Navy.

In 1921, while at the family's vacation home off the Maine coast, Roosevelt became stricken with polio. Initially, he could not even move his arms or legs. But in a courageous, lifetime struggle against the ravaging disease, he fought his way back. Spending long, hard hours swimming and exercising, he slowly regained the use of his hands and arms. While he was never again able to walk without the use of crutches and braces on his legs, he managed to develop extremely powerful arms and shoulders.

Roosevelt was elected Governor of New York in 1928, and four years later he won the Presidential election. By the time he took office, the Depression had deepened, and Roosevelt took immediate action to restore the public's confidence. He pledged a "New Deal," devoted to relief, recovery, and reform. Working with Congress during the first "100 Days," Roosevelt oversaw the passing of a mass of legislation, the extent and implications of which have never been matched before or since.

Attempting to strengthen the financial and business structure, Roosevelt first ordered the four day closing of banks to halt depositor panic and cut government expenditures. To calm the citizens of the country, he began a series of radio "fireside chats" in order to explain and gain public support for his programs.

Among the legislation passed during the "100 Days" was the creation of the Federal Deposit Insurance Corporation (FDIC), which safeguarded bank deposits; the Civilian Conservation Corps (CCC), which put thousands of young men to work on conservation projects; the Tennessee Valley Authority (TVA), which placed the Government in the power business and initiated intensified regional planning; and the Public Works Administration (PWA), which employed workers on newly created construction projects.

In 1935, during the "Second New Deal," more significant legislation was enacted. The Works Progress Administration (WPA) (after 1939 the Works Projects Administration), provided Federal jobs for workers, artists, writers, musicians, and actors; the Social Security Act set up a system of Federal and State unemployment compensation, as well as a Federal program of senior citizen and survivors' benefits.

In the election of 1936, Roosevelt carried every state in the Union with the exception of two. In 1938, Roosevelt got Congress to pass legislation calling for higher farm price subsidies, and the Fair Labor Standards Act, which set minimum wages, limited hours, and banned child labor.

By 1939 Roosevelt and the nation had a new problem to face: World War II, which would eventually act to fully bring the country out of its economic depression. In 1940 the Democrats nominated Roosevelt for a third term. He accepted the nomination and won an easy victory, becoming the first and only President to serve three terms. On December 7, 1941, the Japanese bombed Pearl Harbor in Hawaii and the United States was forced to enter into the war.

In 1944, with war still waging, Roosevelt was elected for the fourth time. The only President known to an entire generation of Americans, Roosevelt had shattered the two-term tradition, serving an unprecedented tenure of more than 12 years. But now the unbelievable strain and the long hours of work were wreaking havoc with his health. In the summer and fall of that year, representatives of the United States, Great Britain, the Soviet Union, and China met at Dumbarton Oaks, in Washington, D.C., to draft an agreement for what would become known as the United Nations.

Roosevelt was applauded as the Allies began to take control of the war, but he was robbed of the opportunity to witness the final victory. Only weeks before the war ended in Europe, on April 12, 1945, Roosevelt was resting at his cottage in Warm Springs, Georgia. While an artist was painting his picture, he put a hand to his head and fell backward in his chair. A few hours later he was dead.

HARRY S. TRUMAN
33rd President of the United States, 1945-1953
"Give 'em hell, Harry"

Born: May 8, 1884, Lamar, MO
Died: December 26, 1972, Kansas City, MO

Born in 1884 at Lamar, Missouri, Harry S. Truman was the son of a farmer and livestock dealer. The middle initial "S" in Harry's name was said to have been chosen by his parents to avoid any display of favoritism — his *paternal* grandfather's name was Shippe, and his *maternal* grandfather's name was Solomon.

Harry's father moved his family to Independence when Harry was six years old. By the time Harry was eight years old, he wore extremely thick glasses which necessitated that the boy shy away from athletic pursuits in favor of such less active hobbies as reading and playing the piano. By the age of 14, Truman later said, he had read every book in the town library.

Truman did not attend college because of financial problems. Instead, after graduating from high school, he worked at a series of odd jobs: railroad timekeeper, bookkeeper, mailroom clerk, and bank clerk. When the United States entered World War I, the 33 year old Truman was commissioned as a First Lieutenant in the field artillery, and would go on to take part in many important campaigns.

After the war, Truman, who liked to swear every now and then, enjoy a good poker game, and was known to lose his temper on more than one occasion, came home and married his childhood sweetheart, Elizabeth V. ("Bess") Wallace. They immediately moved into his widowed mother-in-law's home, which would become their primary residence for the remainder of their married lives.

In 1934 Truman was elected to the U.S. Senate. During his second Senate term, he received national acclaim for his investigation into war profiteering, defense expenditures, and military production. In 1944 Truman received the Vice Presidential nomination under Roosevelt. When Roosevelt died in April, 1945, Truman became President, and he immediately encountered a series of major events.

V-E Day, on May 8, 1945, signaled the end of the war in Europe. Truman took part in the peace negotiations, including the Potsdam Conference. After this meeting, Truman was faced with one of the most difficult decisions anyone has ever had to make: Should the United States use its recently developed atomic bomb on Japan? Agreeing with his advisers that it would, in the end, save thousands of American lives, Truman gave orders to drop the bomb. Hiroshima and Nagasaki were destroyed; the war was over on August 14, 1945.

Truman ran for President in 1948, operating what came to be known as the "whistle stop" campaign. The newspapers and the polls predicted that he would be badly defeated by Thomas E. Dewey, the Governor of New York. Truman even went to bed the night of the election thinking that he had lost. But to almost everyone's shock, he pulled off an upset.

During his second term, Truman backed the Marshall Plan, which served as the economic foundation to the rebuilding of Western Europe. His "Point Four" program offered billions of dollars of economic and technical aid to developing nations. And when Communists tried to overthrow the government of Greece, Truman declared that the United States would help any country fighting to stay free of Communism. This commitment was soon known as the Truman Doctrine.

During the Berlin Airlift, Truman ordered a massive amount of supplies flown into the city that was being cut off by the Russians. In June 1950, Communists from Northern Korea invaded the South. Truman responded by sending American troops into the area.

Truman enacted legislation calling for the end of segregation and racial discrimination in the Armed Forces, and helped push through congressional measures ordering increases in the minimum wage, expansion of Social Security benefits, the clearance of slums, the building of public housing, conservation, and the continuation of farm price supports.

In 1952, Truman decided not to seek reelection. He retired to Independence, where he continued to participate in party affairs, wrote his memoirs, and guided the establishment of the Truman Presidential Library. He died in 1972.

DWIGHT D. EISENHOWER
34th President of the United States, 1953-1961
"I Like Ike"

Born: October 14, 1890, Denison, TX
Died: March 28, 1969, Washington, D.C.

Dwight David Eisenhower was born in 1890 in Denison, Texas, moved with his family the following year to Abilene, Kansas, and graduated high school at the age of 19, where he was an average student. A fast, lean, and strong young man, Dwight played both football and baseball; his teammates called him "Ike."

In 1911 he was nominated to West Point, where he graduated in the top third of his class. As a second lieutenant at Fort Sam Houston, in San Antonio, Texas, Eisenhower met Mary G. ("Mamie") Doud of Denver. They got married in 1916, and the couple had two sons, the first one of whom died as an infant. Eisenhower later served on the staffs of General John Pershing and General Douglas MacArthur.

In 1942, shortly after the United States entered World War II, Eisenhower was named as the Assistant Chief of Staff. After drawing up plans for war in the Pacific that were nothing short of extraordinary, President Roosevelt promoted him over 366 other officers to head the U.S. armies in Europe. Later that year, he became the

Commander of the European Theater of Operations, where he orchestrated the invasions of North Africa, Sicily, and Italy — a feat which brought him international fame. Towards the end of 1943, Eisenhower was appointed as the Supreme Allied Commander in Europe, and he led the D-Day invasion of France (June 6, 1944).

After the war Eisenhower retired from the Army and took over the presidency of Columbia University. In 1952, Eisenhower won the United States Presidential election with an easy grin and captivating charm that earned him wide admiration.

Soon after he took over office, Eisenhower flew to Korea, where he helped negotiate a peace settlement. During his Presidency, Eisenhower signed bills that widened Social Security benefits and increased the minimum wage; enacted Federal aid for health and education programs; distributed school lunches at home and foreign aid abroad; and supported funding for a new system of interstate highways.

When the Governor of Arkansas refused to obey the school desegregation decision of the Supreme Court in 1954, Eisenhower called out the Army and forced the Governor to integrate a high school in Little Rock. Later that year, Eisenhower approved the creation of the Civil Rights Commission.

In 1955, Eisenhower suffered a heart attack. Recovering quickly, he ran for a second term and was reelected by a huge majority. Towards the end of 1957, Eisenhower was temporarily hospitalized with a mild stroke. Once again making a strong recovery, he sought detente by inviting Soviet Premier Nikita S. Krushchev to tour the United States and discuss various issues at Camp David, Maryland. In 1960, these diplomatic overtures came to a halt when an American U-2 reconnaissance jet was shot down inside Russia and Khrushchev abruptly ended a Paris summit meeting and cancelled a trip to Russia that Eisenhower was soon to embark upon.

By the end of his second term, Eisenhower was 70 years old, the oldest man at that time to ever hold the office of Chief Executive. Retiring in 1961, Eisenhower spent his last years at his Gettysburg farm. He died in 1969.

JOHN F. KENNEDY
35th President of the United States, 1961-1963
"The New Frontier"

Born: May 29, 1917, Brookline, MA
Died: November 22, 1963, Dallas, TX

The second child and second son of nine children, John Fitzgerald Kennedy was born in 1917 in Brookline Massachusetts, a suburb of Boston. His father, Joseph P. Kennedy, built a multimillion dollar fortune in business and finance, and served as President Roosevelt's chairman of the Securities and Exchange Commission (1934-35) and Ambassador to Great Britain (1935-40); he gave each of his children a million dollars when they turned 21 years of age. John's mother was a well-educated member of a prominent, highly political Irish-American family.

Kennedy earned his B.S. degree from Harvard University in 1940 with honors in political science. His senior thesis, *Why England Slept*, became a best-seller. When World War II began, Kennedy joined the Navy and commanded PT-109, a motor-torpedo patrol boat, in the South Pacific. During a fierce battle at night, a Japanese destroyer rammed and sank his small craft, cutting it in half. Two men were killed and Kennedy's back was badly injured. Despite this injury, Kennedy swam for hours, towing another man even more badly hurt than he to a nearby island. He was awarded the Purple Heart and the Navy and Marine Corps Medal.

In 1946, with nearly every member of his family campaigning for him, he was elected to the U.S. House of Representatives. In 1948 and 1950 he easily won reelection.

Kennedy married Jacqueline Lee Bouvier in 1953. She was to give birth to one daughter and two sons, one of whom died shortly after birth.

Profiles in Courage, Kennedy's book about United States Senators who had risked their careers to fight for causes they believed in, won the Pulitzer Prize for biography.

In 1960, the 43 year old Kennedy ran against Richard M. Nixon for President. The campaign featured the first televised debate between two Presidential candidates. In one of the closest elections in history, Kennedy edged Nixon.

Soon after his inauguration, Kennedy supported an unsuccessful invasion by anti-Communist Cuban exiles of their homeland. The so-called "Bay of Pigs" invasion on April 17, 1961 proved to be a dismal failure, and Kennedy publicly accepted responsibility.

When East Germany constructed a wall to cut off West Berlin from the Communist sector, Kennedy built up U.S. forces in Europe, and two years later delivered his famous "Ich bin ein Berliner" ("I am a Berliner") speech at the wall.

In Ocotober 1962, Kennedy obtained proof that the Soviet Union had placed intermediate-range missiles capable of striking the U.S. mainland in Cuba. During what became known as the "Cuban Missile Crisis" Kennedy announced in an emergency telecast to the Nation that the Navy would blackade Cuba so no more Russian ships could enter. He sent planes and soldiers to Florida to be ready to invade Cuba if necessary. Nuclear war seemed imminent, and for a week the United States and Russia waited for the other to make the first move. Finally, the Russians backed down, and Khrushchev agreed to remove the missiles.

During his brief time as President, Kennedy established the Peace Corps to help under-developed countries, made notable gains in civil rights, and ended religious and racial discrimination in housing built or purchased with federal funds.

Additionally, Kennedy backed the extensive programs his brother, Attorney General Robert F. Kennedy, implemented for the registration of black voters. He sent U.S. marshals and troops to Oxford, Mississippi to enforce the enrollment of the University of Mississippi's first black student, James H. Meredith, and endorsed Martin Luther

King, Jr.'s historic march on Washington, D.C. (1963).

After Alan Shepard's successful suborbital flight in 1961, Kennedy established an imaginative space program whose goal was the landing of a man on the moon by the end of the decade. He would not live long enough to see his dream come true. On November 22, 1963, while riding in an automobile procession from Love Field to the Trade Mart, in Dallas, Texas, along streets lined with cheering spectators, President Kennedy was shot and killed by a gun fired from a sixth-floor window in a building overlooking the procession. He was the fourth President ever to be assassinated. Lee Harvey Oswald, the accused assassin, was murdered two days later in the Dallas Police Station by Jack Ruby (Rubenstein), a Dallas night-club owner.

LYNDON B. JOHNSON
36th President of the United States, 1963-1969
"Great Society"

Born: August 27, 1908, Stonewall, TX
Died: January 22, 1973, San Antonio, TX

Lyndon Johnson was born to be a politician. Both his father and his grandfather had been members of the Texas Legislature, and the day of his birth Lyndon's grandfather mounted his horse and went galloping around the country shouting, "A United States senator has just been born!"

When he graduated high school in 1924, Johnson was six feet three inches tall, skinny, and restless. Heading west for California, he worked an assortment of odd jobs, from elevator operator, to field hand, to cafe worker. The following year, he returned to his Texas home, and spent two more years drifting from job to job. In 1930 he earned his B.S. degree at San Marcos College (now Southwest Texas College). In late 1931, he worked as secretary to Texas Congressman Richard M. Kleberg, and in 1934 he married Claudia Alta ("Lady Bird") Taylor, the daughter of a well-to-do planter-merchant of Marshall, Texas. They were to raise two daughters together.

When Johnson was 29 years old he ran for Congress and was elected. After the Japanese bombed Pearl Harbor, Johnson was the first member of Congress to ask for active duty in the

Navy, and the first to go into uniform. Reelected to five more terms, Johnson sat in the House until 1948, becoming the protege of Majority Leader (later Speaker) Sam Rayburn and President Franklin D. Roosevelt. Johnson was next elected to the U.S. Senate, where he rose rapidly, becoming Majority Whip within three years. In 1953, the 44-year-old Senator was elected as Minority Leader — the youngest in history. In January 1955 he was named as Senate Majority Leader.

Johnson was elected as Kennedy's Vice President in 1960. When President Kennedy was assassinated, Johnson was sworn into office while aboard the Presidential jet in Dallas, only hours after Kennedy had died. Johnson soon initiated the domestic program he called the "Great Society." Included in this plan was the Civil Rights Act of 1964, which outlawed segregation in public accommodations and promoted fair employment practices, and the Voting Rights Act of 1965, which guaranteed blacks the right to vote.

Johnson's War on Poverty aimed to improve city slums and other poor sections of the country. It provided for a food stamp system, and established the Job Corps for the training of unemployed youth. Jonson pushed through a Medicare law, and saw that legislation was passed to slow down the pollution of American rivers and air and to make highways more beautiful. In 1964 he was reelected President by a huge majority.

Johnson's most significant problems were in the area of foreign affairs, especially Southeast Asia. Ever since the end of World War II, Communist revolutionaries supported by the North Vietnamese government had tried to overthrow the government of South Vietnam, an American ally. In 1965, Johnson accelerated participation in the Vietnam War, and over the next few years he gradually increased the number of troops sent to counter Viet Cong and North Vietnamese attacks.

At home, Johnson's Great Society Programs began to suffer because so much money and attention were going to the war in Vietnam. Debate over the war came to divide the United States, with young people especially critical. Antiwar demonstrations took place all across the country, during which American flags and army draft cards were burned. Johnson's administration was also hurt by a series of riots that broke out in many black areas around the United States, as Afro-Americans vented their anger at a host of social and economic grievances and the assassinations of Martin Luther King, Jr. and Malcolm X.

On March 31, 1968, Johnson appeared on television to make a speech that surprised the country: He said, "I shall not seek, and I will not accept, the nomination of my party for another term as your President." Johnson retired to his Texas ranch when his term was over in 1969. He died four years later of a heart attack.

RICHARD M. NIXON
37th President of the United States, 1969-1974
"Watergate"

Born: January 9, 1913, Yorba Linda, CA

Richard M. Nixon was raised by Quaker parents in Yorba Linda and Whittier, California. He graduated from Whittier College, a small school near his home, and then earned a scholarship to Duke University, in North Carolina, where he studied law. While attending Duke, Nixon was elected as president of the student bar association, and eventually graduated with honors in 1937.

Nixon returned to Whittier, was admitted to the bar, and began practicing with a local firm. He met (Thelma C.) Patricia ("Pat") Ryan, a high school business teacher, while acting in an amateur theater group. They were married in 1940, and together they raised two daughters, Julie and "Tricia" (Patricia).

After World War II, Nixon ran for Congress. He served two terms in the House of Representatives and was then elected to the Senate. In 1952, Presidential candidate Dwight Eisenhower selected the 40 year old Nixon as his running mate. After their election, Nixon became the second youngest man to ever hold the office.

In 1960 Nixon ran for President against John Kennedy, and was defeated in one of the closest elections in history. In 1962 he lost a bid for the Governorship of California. After moving to New York City and joining a distinguished law firm, Nixon won the Presidential election of 1968.

In the November 1972 election, Nixon won the largest number of popular votes in the Nation's history. A cease-fire agreement was soon signed with North Vietnam, and in 1973 Nixon helped orchestrate a cease-fire between Israel and Egypt and Syria.

One of the highlights of Nixon's Presidency was his historic trip to Communist China in February, 1972. This bid to open new channels for trade and communications was the first high-level contact between the two nations in decades. Later that same year and in 1974, Nixon journeyed to the Soviet Union, where in a spirit of detente he signed a treaty limiting strategic nuclear weapons.

Domestically, Nixon instituted mandatory wage and price controls; devalued the dollar; and took steps to counter the energy crisis, which intensified when the Arab nations placed an embargo on oil towards the end of 1973. Nixon also made four appointments to the Supreme Court, declared a "war" against crime and narcotics, opposed compulsory busing to desegregate schools, and ended the military draft. Early in his administration, the country watched with joy as American astronauts landed on the moon.

Nixon's second term was cut short by a series of scandals. These began with press revelations that on June 17, 1972, five men were arrested for breaking into the Democratic National Committee headquarters at the Watergate hotel and office building complex in Washington, D.C. At the time of their capture, they possessed electronic surveillance devices and cameras, all part of an eleborate bugging scheme devised, it transpired, by agents of the Committee to Re-elect the President.

As time went on, the "Watergate Affair" came to be associated with a variety of illegal activities on the part of the President and many of his Cabinet members, key aides, and campaign advisers. More trouble came with the announcement that Vice President Spiro Agnew was charged with accepting bribes. In October 1973, Agnew resigned as Vice President, and Congressman Gerald Ford was chosen to replace him.

By the spring of 1974, despite Nixon's insistence that he had known nothing about the burglary and had no part in covering it up, it seemed certain that the House of Representatives would impeach the President, and very likely that the Senate would convict him. Under pressure from his own legal counsel, Nixon surrendered three transcripts of conversations recorded in the White

House a few days after the Watergate break-in. These tapes showed without a doubt that Nixon had not only taken part in the cover-up, but had tried to keep the FBI from investigating. The country was outraged. On August 9, 1974, claiming that he wanted to spare the Nation further stress, Nixon resigned and retired to his home in San Clemente, California. He was subsequently given a full Presidential pardon by his replacement, Vice President Ford.

GERALD R. FORD
38th President of the United States, 1974-1976
"Most Valuable Player"

Born: July 14, 1913, Omaha, NE

Gerald Ford was born Leslie Lynch King, the same name as his father. However, his parents divorced soon after his birth and his mother married a paint salesman named Gerald Rudolph Ford. Ford adopted his baby stepson, and the child's name was changed to Gerald R. Ford, Jr.

Gerald was raised in Grand Rapids, Michigan. Big and strong, he enjoyed sports, participating on the high school football, basketball, and track teams. After graduating in 1931, Ford enrolled at the University of Michigan. Supporting himself through school with such odd jobs as busboy at the university hospital and dishwasher in a fraternity house, he was still able to maintain a "B" average. Ford also managed to play center on the school's national championship football teams of 1932 and 1933. The latter year he was named the team's most valuable player.

Rejecting offers to play professional football, Ford instead joined the athletic staff of Yale University. While serving as an assistant football and boxing coach, he attended law school, where he ranked in the top third of his class. In January

1941 he received his law degree from Yale and returned to Grand Rapids to set up his practice.

When the United States entered World War II, Ford quit law and joined the Navy. Assigned to the light aircraft carrier Monterey, he saw some of the fiercest battles of the war in the Pacific. In 1948 he married Elizabeth Bloomer Warren, a department-store fashion coordinator. They were to raise three sons and one daughter. That same year he ran for Congress, and was elected easily.

In 12 subsequent bids for the same office, Ford routinely received over 60 percent of the vote. During the final eight of his 25 years of service in the House of Representatives (1949-73), he functioned as Minority Leader. In 1973, President Nixon asked Ford to replace Agnew as his Vice President, and on August 9, 1974, upon Nixon's resignation, Ford became the first man to be President without ever having run for the office of either President or Vice President.

One of Ford's first acts, designed to lift the spirits of the psychologically beleaguered Nation, was to grant a full pardon to former President Nixon. Ford also nominated former New York Governor Nelson A. Rockefeller as his Vice President.

Ford's major domestic problem was the economy, which had been ailing since 1973. Weakened by soaring inflation, mounting unemployment, and a worsening energy crisis, the country was experiencing a serious recession. Unfortunately, neither Congress nor the President, who held fundamentally different economic philosophies, was ever able to create anti-recession policies that were acceptable to the other.

Perhaps Ford's most joyous time in office was when he presided over the Nation's Bicentennial celebration, which culminated on July 4, 1976, with festivities all across the country. Later that year, Ford was defeated by Jimmy Carter. In retirement, Ford spent much of his time enjoying such sports as golf and skiing.

JIMMY CARTER
39th President of the United States, 1977-1981
"New Spirit"

Born: October 1, 1924, Plains, GA

James Earl ("Jimmy") Carter, Jr. was born to a farmer-storekeeper and a registered nurse in the small town of Plains, Georgia. As a boy, Jimmy's dream was to be a sailor. After entering the Georgia Institute of Technology ("Georgia Tech") at Atlanta in 1942 as a naval ROTC student, Carter was able to realize his childhood ambition when he was accepted by the U.S. Naval Academy in Annapolis, Maryland. Shortly after graduating 59th in a class of 820, Carter married Rosalynn Smith. They raised four children — three sons and a daughter.

In 1953, when Carter was 29 years old, his father passed away and he was forced to resign from the Navy and return home to run the family farm. He eventually enlarged the farm, bought a cotton gin, and purchased a peanut manufacturing plant.

After winning a seat on the county school board, Carter ran for the State Senate in 1962. He went on to serve there for two terms before losing the 1966 Georgia gubernatorial campaign. In 1970 he ran once again, this time winning the election. During his single term (1971-75) as Governor of Georgia, Carter tightened budget procedures, displayed strong interest in conservation, and attracted national attention for his moderate stance on civil rights.

In 1976, surprising political experts who had originally given him little hope, Carter defeated Ford in the Presidential election, becoming the first President from Georgia and the first elected directly from the deep South since Zachary Taylor in 1848.

Carter's first major act as President was his pardon of draft evaders of the Vietnam War period. But it was his crusade for human rights both at home and in such countries as the Soviet Union, that attracted worldwide attention. Carter limited or completely banned U.S. aid and exports to nations whose governments were shown to be violating human rights.

While the nation's economy improved and unemployment fell during Carter's first year in office, 1978 brought high levels of inflation. The oil-producing countries in the Middle East raised their prices, and as the cost of oil continued to climb, so did the price of almost everything else. Interest rates rose so high, few people could afford to borrow money to build new homes or buy new equipment, and businesses were unable to borrow the capital necessary to expand.

In an attempt to fight inflation, Carter urged businesses to avoid major price increases and asked labor leaders to keep wage demands to a minimum. But these steps had little effect on inflation, and Carter suffered a sharp drop in his performance rating in public opinion.

To make matters worse, in February 1979, a movement led by Ayatollah Ruhollah Khomeini, a Muslim religious leader, overthrew the United States-friendly government of the Shah of Iran. Iranian revolutionaries stormed the United States Embassy in Teheran, the capital of the country, seizing a group of U.S. citizens, most of whom were embassy employees, and holding them as hostages for 444 days. In exchange for the prisoners, the revolutionaries demended that the United States return the Shah to Iran so that he could be placed on trial.

In April 1980, Carter ordered the military to attempt a secret rescue. However, this operation failed when several helicopters crashed in a desert dust storm, killing eight marines. In July 1980, a public opinion poll showed that only 21 per cent of Americans approved of Carter's performance, the lowest score on record for any President.

The Iranian revolutionaries finally released the Americans on January 20, 1981, the day Carter left office.

Earlier in his administration, Carter did score a triumph in another part of the Middle East. In 1978, he arranged meetings at Camp David in the United States between himself and President

Anwar el-Sadat of Egypt and Prime Minister Menachem Begin of Israel. At this conference Carter helped work out a major agreement called the Camp David Accord (1979), which guaranteed peace between Israel and Egypt. It was the high point of Carter's Presidency.

In late 1979 and early 1980, the Soviet Union invaded Afghanistan, and Soviet-American relations plunged to their lowest point in years. At Carter's urging, the United States and many other nations refused to participate in the 1980 Summer Olympic Games in Moscow as a protest against the invasion. Carter also asked the U.S. Senate to postpone consideration of the SALT I treaty, an agreement somewhat limiting the creation of new nuclear weapons which he had signed with Soviet President Leonid Brezhnev earlier in his administration.

When Carter ran for reelection in 1980 against Ronald Reagan, he was defeated by a landslide. Returning to Plains after leaving office, Carter wrote books and remained active in national and international issues. In 1989, George Bush sent Carter to Panama to help monitor that country's Presidential election. In 1990, Carter led a team of observers that monitored the Presidential election in Nicaragua.

RONALD REAGAN
40th President of the United States, 1981-1989
"The Great Communicator"

Born: February 6, 1911, Tampico, IL

Ronald Reagan was born on February 6, 1911, in Tampico, Illinois to his shoe salesman father and his shop clerk mother. As a boy, Ronald's family lived in a number of small Illinois towns. His mother, Nelle Reagan, loved the theater and was an actress in many amateur productions. As a result, Ronald became interested in performing at an early age. He also enjoyed fishing, swimming, and playing football.

In 1928, Reagan entered Eureka College, a small school near his home. He put himself through college with a partial scholarship, savings from a lifeguard job, and money he earned washing dishes at a fraternity house. Among his early accomplishments were memberships on the football, track, and swimming team, as well as leading roles in several college plays. He also became president of the student body.

After graduating, Reagan was hired as a sports announcer for a radio station. In 1937, when he was 26 years old, he traveled to California to cover baseball's spring training. While in California a friend got him a screen test at Warner Brothers, and the studio signed him to a contract.

Reagan soon became a movie star, known for his roles as a wholesome, likable young man. In *Knute Rockne — All American* (1940), Reagan gained fame playing college football star George (the Gipper) Gipp. Between 1937 and 1964, Reagan would appear in more than 50 features. The actor met actress Jane Wyman while they both were appearing in films for Warner Brothers, and they were married in 1940. The couple had a daughter and a son before divorcing in 1948.

In 1947, Reagan became president of the Screen Actors Guild (SAG), and became involved in a dispute between his union and other unions in the movie-making business. He was elected to five consecutive terms, serving until 1952. During this period, in 1951, he met actress Nancy Davis. She and Reagan were married in 1954, and the couple had two children.

Reagan first gained national political attention during the 1964 Presidential campaign, when he made a rousing televised speech on behalf of the Republican candidate, Barry M. Goldwater. Two years later, Reagan ran for Governor of California, winning the election easily, and going on to serve two terms.

In 1968, while still Governor, he unsuccessfully challenged Richard Nixon for his party's Presidential nomination. In 1976 Reagan faced a similar fate against Gerald Ford. Finally, in 1980,

Reagan won the nomination, and at 69 years of age — the oldest man ever to be elected — he went on to win the Presidential election.

As President, Reagan, certain that tax cuts would improve business, pushed several of these measures through Congress. In order to save the government money, he asked Congress for heavy cuts in programs that aided the poor, the aged, the environment, and the national parks, among others. Newspapers and magazines called his economic policies "Reaganomics."

At the same time, Reagan asked for and received record amounts of money for the military. Convinced of the worldwide threat of Communism, he sent military advisers and millions of dollars to help defend the Central American governments of El Salvador and Honduras against Communist rebels, and to oppose the Communist-influenced government of Nicaragua. Additionally, he sent U.S. troops to Lebanon where, with the help of British, French, and Italian soldiers, they were to act as a "peace-keeping force" in the Middle East.

Public criticism of many of Reagan's appointments and domestic policies began to grow. The President's major critics included the millions of Americans, especially blacks, women, and environmentalists, who suffered from unemployment and reductions in social and environmental programs.

In March 1981, an attempt was made on Reagan's life in Washington, D.C. Despite being shot in the chest, Reagan made a full recovery. John W. Hinckley, Jr. was charged with the shooting, and in 1982, a jury declared that Hinckley was insane at the time of the attempted assassination and, therefore, found him not guilty of the murder charge. A federal judge later ordered Hinckley to be placed in a mental institution.

In October 1983, bombs set off by a terrorist killed 241 U.S. troops who were headquartered in a building at the airport in Beirut, Lebanon.

In 1984 Reagan was reelected by a landslide. He immediately began to press for funds to develop the Strategic Defense Initiative (SDI), a space-based anti-missile shield whose aim was to protect the United States against nuclear attack. The newspapers referred to the program as "Star Wars." In addition, Reagan asked Congress to rewrite the tax laws, creating a new, simplified tax system, and he met with Soviet Leader Mikhail Gorbachev in Switzerland (1985) and Iceland (1986). In 1987, Gorbachev visited Reagan in the United States, where the two leaders signed a treaty that called for the destruction of all medium-range, ground-launched U.S. and Soviet nuclear missiles.

Reagan repeatedly stated that he would make no bargains to secure the release of Americans kidnapped by terrorists in Beirut. So the nation was shocked when a Beirut magazine reported in November 1986 that former National Security Advisor Robert McFarlane had been in Iran negotiating a secret arms shipment. The arms sales were chiefly designed to win the freedom of the American hostages. When news that the profits from the sales had apparently been diverted to the Contras in Nicaragua — to whom Congress had banned military aid — the image of Reagan's administration suffered a further blow.

The Iran-contra Affair grew into a national scandal, with Congress forming a special committee to investigate the matter. Later in 1987, Reagan was strongly criticized by the committee for failing to meet his constitutional obligation to "take care that the laws be faithfully executed."

In October 1987 the stock market plunged, signaling that Reagan's financial policies were in serious trouble. The increased social and military spending backed by the President and Congress had resulted in huge budget deficits, and the United States was now the biggest debtor nation in the world.

After leaving the White House, Reagan retired to Bel Air, California, where he continued to deliver speeches in support of a variety of conservative causes.

GEORGE BUSH
41st President of the United States, 1989-
"Operation Desert Storm"

Born: June 12, 1924, Milton, MA.

George's father was a successful businessman who went on to become a managing partner in a New York investment banking firm. He later represented Connecticut in the United States Senate from 1952 to 1963.

After graduating in 1942 from Phillips Academy at Andover, Massachusetts — where he was president of the senior class and captain of the baseball and soccer teams — Bush had intended on enrolling in Yale University. But when the United States entered World War II, he chose to delay his college education and instead enlisted in the U.S. Naval Reserve. He received flight training and was commissioned an ensign in June 1943, becoming the Navy's youngest pilot at that time.

On September 2, 1944, Bush's plane was shot down during an attack on a Japanese-held island, but not before Bush scored damaging hits on a key radio station. A United States submarine rescued Bush from the ocean, and he was subsequently awarded the Distinguished Flying Cross for his heroism.

While attending a Christmas dance in 1941, Bush met Barbara Pierce, whose father, Marvin Pierce, was the publisher of the popular *McCall's* and *Redbook* magazines. Married in 1945, the couple raised six children, one of whom died as a child.

In 1945 Bush entered Yale University, graduating Phi Beta Kappa three years later with a bachelor's degree in economics. In 1962, after a successful career in the oil business, Bush was elected chairman of the Republican Party of Harris County, Texas. In 1966, Bush ran for the U.S. House of Representatives, and defeated his opponent. He was reelected to the House without opposition in 1968.

President Nixon appointed Bush as the U.S. Ambassador to the United Nations in December 1970. Two years later, President Nixon appointed Bush as the chairman of the Republican National Committee. In November 1975, at President Ford's request, Bush headed the Central Intelligence Agency. Five years later, Ronald Reagan invited Bush to be his Vice Presidential running mate.

In 1988, Bush defeated Michael S. Dukakis in the Presidential election. Early in his Presidency, Bush had to contend with the worst crisis in the savings and loan industry since the Great Depression. Over the course of the 1980s, more than 21,000 of these institutions had failed and hundreds more teetered on the edge of bankruptcy.

Soon after entering office, Bush proposed legislation to rescue and restructure the industry.

In September 1989, Bush proposed a new federal strategy for reducing the use of illegal drugs in the United States. This so-called "War on Drugs" called for stronger law enforcement efforts against the users of illegal drugs, and increased efforts to reduce production of such drugs at home and abroad. In December 1989, Bush sent U.S. troops into Panama to overthrow the dictatorship of General Manuel Antonio Noriega. The following month, Noriega surrendered to officials and was taken to the United States to face trial on drug trafficking charges.

In June 1990, Bush met with Soviet leader Mikhail Gorbachev, and agreed to destroy approximately one third of their countries' long-range nuclear missiles, as well as the majority of their chemical weapons.

In August 1990, after Iraq invaded and took over Kuwait, an oil-rich country between Iraq and Saudi Arabia, Bush ordered tens of thousands of U.S. troops into the area. Additionally, Bush ordered U.S. Navy ships to enforce an embargo on the shipment of goods to and from Iraq. In January 1991, when Iraqi President Saddam Hussein refused to comply with a U.N. resolution calling for the immediate withdrawal of Iraqi forces from Kuwait, the United States and its allies declared war on Iraq.